Rise and Reign:

The Female Leaders' Guide to Health, Life, and Success.

Written by

Dr. Tasheema Fair

Published by Franklin Publishers

Printed in the United States of America

For permissions, inquiries, or additional copies, contact:

Franklin Publishers

www.franklinpublishers.com

Acknowledgments

To my mentors, Dr. Anthony Royek, Pastor Alan and Terri Crider, and Pastor Darryl and Carmisha Arnold – thank you for pouring your wisdom, guidance, and unwavering belief into me. Your mentorship has been a guiding light, shaping my journey and pushing me to achieve more than I ever imagined. I am forever grateful for your leadership and for the invaluable lessons you've imparted.

To my best friends, Regina Chaney, Donethia Nowlin, Gregory Wilson Jr., Christopher Webb, and Taloni Lynn – you are the pillars of my support system, my cheerleaders, and my chosen family. Your love, encouragement, and enduring faith in me have been a source of strength throughout this journey. Thank you for standing beside me, lifting me up, and reminding me of my purpose.

This book would not have been possible without each of you. You have my deepest gratitude and love.

Dedications

To my mother, Julia Beck, whose unwavering love and strength have been my greatest inspiration.

To my stepfather, Perry Beck, for your steadfast support and encouragement, always reminding me of my potential.

To my late father, Jerel Fair, whose memory continues to light my path and inspire me to reach for the stars.

To my brother, Jerel Fair, Jr., for your constant support and the bond we share, that means the world to me.

And to my nieces, Tianna Fair and Aisha Fair, whose joy, energy, and bright futures remind me why every step forward matters.

This book is a testament to your love, guidance, and the indelible impact you've had on my life. Thank you for being my foundation and my motivation.

Introduction

The purpose of Rise and Reign: The Female Leaders' Guide to Health, Life, and Success is to equip you with the strategies to truly thrive, not just survive, in every area of your life. As a female leader, you navigate a world full of demands, expectations, and pressures that can leave you feeling out of balance. This book is your roadmap to creating a life where you can excel in your career without sacrificing your well-being.

Here, we'll explore how mastering your health, life, and business isn't just important—it's essential for living up to your fullest potential. You'll learn how to strengthen yourself physically, mentally, and spiritually, build a life that supports your goals, and run your business in a way that reflects your values. Each chapter is filled with practical tools and personal lessons that I've gathered from my own experiences and the journeys of other women who have found their path to transformation.

This isn't about perfection or quick fixes; it's about making intentional changes that create real, lasting growth. You have the power to shape your life into something extraordinary, and this book will show you how to take that next step with confidence and purpose.

Mastering health, life, and business isn't just a goal; it's a necessity for female leaders who want to make a lasting impact. We often find ourselves juggling countless responsibilities, pouring energy into our careers, families, and communities—sometimes at the expense of our own well-being. However, true leadership starts with taking care of the whole person. When we neglect our health, struggle to balance life's demands, or lose clarity in business, it affects everything we do.

For female leaders, mastering these three areas means building a strong foundation that supports every aspect of who we are. It's about being fit physically, mentally, and spiritually so we have the stamina and resilience to lead with strength. It's about crafting a life that doesn't just work on paper but brings real fulfillment. And it's about driving our businesses with intention, knowing how to deliver value while staying true to our principles.

The stakes are high because the people who rely on us—our teams, families, and communities—need us at our best. When we take control of our health, shape our lives intentionally, and steer our businesses with purpose, we not only elevate ourselves but also inspire others to do the same. That's why mastering these three areas is more than important—it's the key to living and leading with the power, purpose, and passion we were meant to embody.

The journey laid out in this book is about real transformation—a process that requires commitment, courage, and the willingness to make changes from the inside out. As you move through these teachings, you'll discover what it means to become a leader who not only excels but thrives. This journey is about more than reaching goals; it's about reshaping the way you live, work, and lead so that each step forward is grounded in purpose.

You can expect to dig deep and confront the areas where you've been out of balance, overlooked your well-being, or played small in your business. This book will challenge you to rethink your approach to health, life, and leadership, showing you practical ways to bring all three into alignment. You'll learn to tap into the strength that comes from being spiritually centered, mentally resilient, and physically strong. You'll build a life that supports your growth and success instead of draining your energy. And you'll lead your business with clarity and conviction, staying true to your values while reaching new heights.

Transformation isn't a destination; it's a continuous journey of becoming the best version of yourself. Through the lessons and strategies in these pages, you'll gain the tools to keep growing, keep pushing forward, and keep rising to your fullest potential—no matter where you start. This is your invitation to embrace the transformation, not just as a leader, but as a whole person.

Table of Contents

Part III

Master Your Business

Part I

Chapter 1

Health is 3-Dimensional

As women, especially those in leadership, we often focus on just one or two aspects of our well-being—usually the ones that seem to matter most in the moment. Maybe you're working hard to stay physically fit, hitting the gym, or following a diet, but mentally and emotionally, you feel drained. Or perhaps you're investing in your spiritual health, connecting deeply with your faith, but your body feels neglected, and your energy is low. It's easy to feel out of balance when we're only nurturing parts of ourselves.

The truth is that health isn't one-dimensional. It's not just about how your body feels or looks. It's about how your mind operates under stress and how your spirit sustains you when life feels overwhelming. This is why health is 3-dimensional—it's physical, mental, and spiritual. These three areas are interconnected, and when you strengthen all of them, you create the kind of balance that allows you to lead with confidence, resilience, and purpose.

Think of it like this: if one part of you is out of sync, it will affect everything else. You can be in great shape physically, but if your mental health is suffering, you'll still struggle. You might have a strong spiritual practice, but if you're not taking care of your body, it will be hard to show up fully in your leadership. To truly thrive as a female leader, you have to be intentional about nurturing all three dimensions of your health.

Physical Health: Your Body is Your Foundation

Let's start with the physical. As leaders, we put many demands on our bodies. Long hours, high stress, constant travel, and often too little sleep can take their toll. And yet, many of us push our physical health to the back burner, assuming that as long as we can keep going, we're fine. But over time, this neglect can show up in ways that make it hard to lead effectively—whether it's chronic fatigue, illness, or even just a lack of energy and focus.

Taking care of your body doesn't have to mean following the latest diet craze or spending hours in the gym. It's about finding what works for you and making physical health a priority in your everyday life. It's about fueling your body with nutritious food, staying active in ways that you enjoy, and making rest and recovery part of your routine. Remember, your body is the vessel that carries you through everything you do, and when you take care of it, you're better equipped to handle the demands of leadership.

Mental Health: The Power of a Resilient Mind

Next, let's talk about mental health. As a female leader, your mind is one of your greatest assets. It's what allows you to think critically, make decisions, solve problems, and navigate the challenges that come with leading others. But mental health is often the area we overlook, especially when we're juggling so many responsibilities. We push through stress, anxiety, and burnout because we feel we don't have the time to stop and take care of our minds.

Mental fitness is just as important as physical fitness. It's about being mindful of what you allow into your mental space, whether it's the information you consume, the conversations you have, or the self-talk that plays in your head. Just like you exercise your body, you can train your mind to be resilient in the face of challenges. This means learning how to manage stress, staying present in the moment, and developing the ability to bounce back from setbacks.

A big part of mental fitness is also about setting boundaries—knowing when to say no, when to step away, and when to protect your peace. The stronger your mental health, the better equipped you'll be to lead with clarity and focus, even when the pressure is on.

Spiritual Health: Staying Grounded in Your Purpose

Finally, there's spiritual health. This is the dimension that gives everything else meaning. For many of us, spirituality is what sustains us when life gets hard—it's where we find hope, direction, and strength to keep going when nothing else seems to work. But just like the other areas of health, spiritual well-being requires intentional care and practice.

Spiritual health can look different for everyone. It's about staying connected to your higher purpose, whether that's through your faith, meditation, nature, or whatever brings you closer to the Source that guides you. For me, it's my relationship with God. Staying connected to Him through prayer, worship, and reflection is what keeps me grounded, especially during tough times.

When your spiritual health is strong, it becomes the anchor that holds you steady in life's storms. It helps you keep perspective when things get overwhelming and gives you the strength to lead with integrity and compassion. Just like you wouldn't let your body go without nourishment, don't let your spirit go without the attention it needs.

Bringing It All Together: The Balance of 3-Dimensional Health

The real power of 3-dimensional health comes when you bring all three areas—physical, mental, and spiritual—into balance. It's not about perfection; it's about being intentional. When you're taking care of your body, keeping your mind sharp, and staying grounded in your spiritual practice, you create a solid foundation for yourself. This balance gives you the energy, clarity, and resilience you need to lead effectively and live fully.

As a female leader, the stakes are high. You have people depending on you, both in your personal life and in your work. But before you can show up for them, you have to show up for yourself. Health is the key to showing up fully. And when you master 3-dimensional health, you not only elevate your own life but inspire those around you to do the same.

$$******$$

Case Study and Scientific Support on 3-Dimensional Health in Leadership

Arianna Huffington's journey vividly illustrates the power of three-dimensional health in leadership. Huffington, a high-powered media executive and founder of The Huffington Post, was living a life that many would call "successful"—she was leading a top media company, managing a demanding workload, and achieving remarkable career milestones. Yet, in 2007, she faced a major wake-up call. After collapsing from exhaustion and fracturing her cheekbone, she realized that her relentless work habits were harming her well-being and overall effectiveness as a leader.

This incident prompted Huffington to reevaluate her lifestyle and the very definition of success. She began prioritizing her physical, mental, and spiritual health, transforming her life and, ultimately, her leadership style. She established Thrive Global, a company dedicated to promoting well-being and preventing burnout, where she advocates for a holistic approach to health in leadership. Her story exemplifies the importance of nurturing physical, mental, and spiritual health as the foundation for strong and sustainable leadership.

Physical Health: The Essential Foundation for Leadership Stamina

After her health scare, Huffington placed a high priority on physical wellness. She became a vocal advocate for sleep, sharing in her book Thrive that sufficient rest is not only crucial for health but also for cognitive performance and emotional stability. She introduced routines to optimize her physical well-being, such as turning off electronic devices before bed to improve sleep quality and taking time each day for restorative practices like yoga. According to research, sleep directly impacts cognitive functions, including memory, decision-making, and emotional regulation—all crucial for effective leadership (Walker, 2017). Leaders who neglect their physical health may find it harder to manage stress, make clear decisions, and respond calmly to challenges, making physical health a cornerstone of three-dimensional wellness.

Mental Health: Resilience and Focus in the Face of Challenges

Huffington's transformation extended beyond her physical health to include her mental well-being. She introduced mindfulness practices into her daily routine, which she credits for improving her focus and resilience. By managing stress intentionally, she could navigate the demands of leadership with greater clarity and calm. Studies support the impact of mental health on leadership, with evidence showing that mindfulness improves cognitive flexibility, emotional intelligence, and resilience in stressful situations (Good et al., 2016). Leaders who cultivate mental fitness are not only better equipped to manage their own stress but also to lead with empathy and responsiveness, inspiring those they lead.

Spiritual Health: Grounding Leadership in Purpose

Spiritual health became a guiding force for Huffington, helping her find purpose and stay true to her values. She shares in Thrive that connecting to her spirituality gave her a source of strength during times of difficulty. Her approach is echoed by research showing that leaders with a strong sense of purpose and connection to a higher meaning experience greater life satisfaction and are often perceived as more authentic and inspiring by those they lead. Whether it's through prayer, meditation, or a sense of connectedness to something larger, spiritual health provides leaders with a grounding force that allows them to lead with integrity and compassion.

Scientific Support for 3-Dimensional Health in Leadership

The science behind the effectiveness of three-dimensional health is robust. Numerous studies have shown that physical health, mental resilience, and spiritual well-being are essential for sustainable leadership:

1. **Physical Health:** According to a study published in Sleep Health, sleep directly impacts cognitive function, particularly in areas related to memory, learning, and problem-solving (Walker, 2017). Physical activity is also shown to improve energy levels and reduce symptoms of depression, further enhancing leadership capability (Ratey & Loehr, 2011).

2. **Mental Health:** Research by Good et al. (2016) in the Journal of Management found that mindfulness training increased cognitive flexibility and decreased emotional exhaustion in high-stress environments. This is especially relevant for leaders who frequently face challenging decisions and need to manage multiple responsibilities.

3. **Spiritual Health:** A study published in The Leadership Quarterly highlights how spiritual well-being can enhance resilience and adaptability in leaders (Krause et al., 2017). Leaders who engage in spiritual practices are often perceived as more authentic, making it easier for them to inspire and engage their teams.

Through her own experience, Huffington demonstrates that when leaders prioritize these three dimensions of health, they don't just improve their personal well-being—they also increase their ability to lead effectively, inspiring those around them to pursue a more balanced and fulfilling life.

References

- Good, D. J., Lyddy, C. J., Glomb, T. M., Bono, J. E., Brown, K. W., Duffy, M. K., ... & Lazar, S. W. (2016). Contemplating mindfulness at work: An integrative review. *Journal of Management, 42(1), 114-142.*

- Ratey, J. J., & Loehr, J. E. (2011). The positive impact of physical fitness on academic achievement and workplace performance. *Harvard Business Review.*

- Walker, M. P. (2017). Why We Sleep: Unlocking the Power of Sleep and Dreams. New York: Scribner.

Chapter 2

Healthy Spirituality

For any leader, a strong sense of purpose and grounding is essential, especially when facing the inevitable challenges and pressures that come with leadership. Yet, in the pursuit of success, it's easy to lose touch with the deeper aspects of who we are. Spiritual well-being provides a compass—a way to stay rooted in our values, our purpose, and the vision we have for our lives.

For me, spirituality is more than just a practice; it's the foundation that supports everything else I do. It gives me the clarity to make hard decisions, the strength to overcome obstacles, and the wisdom to lead with integrity and compassion. When we invest in our spiritual health, we build resilience and clarity that allow us to show up as authentic, grounded leaders. This chapter is dedicated to exploring what healthy spirituality looks like and how it can empower you to lead with strength and purpose.

The Importance of Spiritual Health in Leadership

Spiritual health is often overlooked in discussions about wellness and leadership, but its impact is profound. When leaders connect with their spiritual well-being, they tap into a source of inner strength that isn't dependent on external success or the approval of others. Spiritual health is what helps us stay focused when distractions are everywhere, calm when chaos surrounds us, and resilient when we're under pressure.

Leadership can sometimes feel isolating, especially when making tough decisions. In those moments, it's spiritual health that offers guidance and comfort, giving us the assurance that we're not alone and that our actions align with something greater than ourselves. This connection to something higher helps us lead with courage, stay grounded in our values, and inspire others with authenticity.

Healthy spirituality is about more than just going through the motions. It's about intentionally connecting with what you believe and allowing it to shape your life and leadership. Whether through prayer, meditation, spending time in nature, or whatever brings you peace, nurturing your spiritual health helps you develop the inner strength and clarity you need to be an effective leader.

Staying Grounded in Purpose and Values

When we don't take the time to nurture our spiritual health, it's easy to lose sight of our purpose and values. As leaders, we face countless distractions and demands on our time, and without a strong spiritual foundation, we risk becoming reactive or disconnected from what truly matters. When we are spiritually healthy, however, we have a stronger sense of purpose. We know why we're doing what we're doing, and that purpose shapes how we lead.

Purpose-driven leadership means making decisions that align with our values, even when it's difficult. It's about staying true to who we are and what we believe, no matter the circumstances. When we're connected to our spiritual health, we're able to lead with confidence, knowing that our actions are aligned with something meaningful. This alignment brings a sense of calm and stability to our leadership, which those around us can see and feel.

Being grounded in purpose also means recognizing that leadership isn't just about personal achievement—it's about serving others. Spiritual health reminds us that our role as leaders is to lift others, inspire them, and create an environment where they can thrive. By focusing on service and staying true to our purpose, we can create a positive impact that goes far beyond our immediate goals.

Developing Practices That Nourish Spiritual Health

Cultivating spiritual health doesn't require grand gestures. It's about finding practices that resonate with you and incorporating them into your daily life. These practices can be as simple as setting aside time for reflection, journaling, or being in nature. The key is consistency—making time each day to reconnect with what matters most to you.

For me, prayer is an essential part of nurturing my spiritual health. Taking a few minutes each morning to center myself in prayer helps me start the day with clarity and focus. I also make time for reflection, whether it's reading scripture or simply sitting quietly to think about what I'm grateful for. These moments of connection ground me, helping me approach each day with purpose and peace.

Another powerful practice is meditation, which helps quiet the mind and create space for reflection. Meditation allows us to step back from the noise of everyday life and connect with our inner selves. Many leaders find that meditation helps them stay calm under pressure, make clearer decisions, and lead with empathy.

You don't have to follow a specific tradition or ritual to develop a strong spiritual practice. What matters most is that you create time and space to connect with yourself and with what you believe. By making spiritual practices a part of your routine, you strengthen the foundation that supports your life and leadership.

Leading with Compassion and Integrity

A strong spiritual foundation allows leaders to lead with compassion and integrity. When we're connected to our spiritual health, we approach leadership with a sense of humility and respect for others. We recognize that everyone we lead has their own challenges, their own hopes, and their own journey. This understanding helps us lead with empathy, treating people with kindness and respect even in difficult situations.

Compassionate leadership doesn't mean avoiding tough decisions; it means making those decisions with a genuine concern for others. It's about being fair, listening to those around us, and recognizing the value that each person brings. Spiritual health reminds us that leadership is not just about results—it's about relationships. When we lead with compassion, we build trust and create a positive, supportive environment where people feel valued and inspired.

Integrity is another key component of spiritually grounded leadership. Leaders who are spiritually healthy are more likely to act with integrity because they are guided by a strong sense of purpose and values. They make decisions that align with their beliefs, even when it's challenging. Integrity builds trust, and trust is essential for effective leadership. When we lead with integrity, we create a culture of honesty and respect, which inspires those around us to do the same.

Spiritual Health as a Source of Resilience

Leadership comes with challenges, and resilience is essential to navigate them. Spiritual health provides an inner strength that helps us stay resilient when times are tough. It gives us the perspective to see beyond immediate setbacks and remain hopeful, knowing that every challenge is an opportunity for growth.

When we're spiritually healthy, we can approach difficulties with a sense of calm and confidence, trusting that we have the inner resources to handle whatever comes our way. Spiritual resilience allows us to maintain a positive outlook, even when faced with obstacles. It helps us stay patient, compassionate, and focused, which not only strengthens our own leadership but also inspires others to stay resilient.

Spiritual health teaches us that we are more than our roles, our successes, or our failures. This understanding allows us to maintain perspective and keep going, even when things don't go as planned. Resilience isn't about ignoring challenges; it's about having the strength to face them with faith and determination.

Embracing Spiritual Health as a Lifelong Journey

Healthy spirituality isn't something you achieve overnight—it's a lifelong journey of growth and self-discovery. There will be times when it's easy to feel connected and other times when it feels challenging. But by committing to nurturing your spiritual health, you build a foundation that will sustain you through the ups and downs of leadership.

As leaders, our spiritual health is not just a personal matter; it's something that impacts everyone around us. When we're grounded, compassionate, and resilient, we create a positive influence that extends to our teams, our families, and our communities. Embracing spiritual health is one of the greatest gifts we can give to ourselves and to those we lead.

The journey to healthy spirituality is ongoing, but it's one of the most rewarding paths we can take. As you continue to nurture your spiritual health, you'll find that it not only strengthens your leadership but also brings a deeper sense of meaning and fulfillment to every aspect of your life.

******

Techniques and Habits for Nurturing Spiritual Health

Nurturing spiritual health is about creating intentional practices that connect you with your values, deepen your sense of purpose, and bring inner peace. Spirituality doesn't have a one-size-fits-all formula; it's a personal journey that should feel genuine and meaningful to you. As leaders, cultivating spiritual health isn't just a matter of finding tranquility in our own lives—it's a source of strength that enables us to inspire and serve others with authenticity and compassion.

Below are techniques and habits that can help you build a strong foundation of spiritual health. These practices are flexible and can be adapted to fit your unique lifestyle and beliefs. The key is consistency: by incorporating these practices into your daily or weekly routine, you create space to reconnect with your purpose and stay grounded, even when life feels overwhelming.

1. Morning Reflection: Starting the Day with Purpose

One of the most powerful habits for nurturing spiritual health is a morning reflection practice. Taking a few quiet moments each morning to center yourself can set the tone for your entire day. During this time, you can reflect on what you're grateful for, your intentions for the day, and any spiritual guidance or inspiration you may need.

This reflection doesn't need to be long; even five or ten minutes of quiet can make a difference. For some, this may take the form of prayer, meditation, or reading an inspiring passage. For others, it might mean sitting quietly with a cup of coffee, breathing deeply, and thinking about the day ahead. This simple habit helps you approach the day with clarity and focus, reminding you of your purpose before the demands of the day take over.

2. Gratitude Practice: Cultivating a Spirit of Thankfulness

Gratitude is a transformative practice that shifts your focus from what's missing to what you have. When you make time each day to recognize and appreciate the blessings in your life, you not only nurture your spiritual health but also increase your resilience and sense of contentment.

You might consider keeping a gratitude journal, writing down three things you're grateful for each day. These don't have to be grand gestures;

they can be as simple as a good conversation, a moment of laughter, or a quiet evening at home. Over time, this practice helps you cultivate a mindset of thankfulness, making it easier to stay positive and grounded, even when challenges arise.

3. Meditation: Building Inner Peace and Clarity

Meditation is a powerful tool for connecting with your inner self and calming the mind. By creating a daily meditation practice, even if only for a few minutes, you give yourself the gift of stillness in a world that often demands constant action and attention. Meditation helps reduce stress, improve focus, and build emotional resilience—all of which are essential for effective leadership.

You don't have to be an expert or commit to long sessions to benefit from meditation. Start small, with five minutes of deep breathing or a guided meditation, and gradually increase as you become more comfortable. Apps like Calm or Headspace offer guided meditations tailored for beginners, helping you establish a routine. This practice not only benefits your spiritual health but also enhances your overall well-being, making it easier to lead with patience and clarity.

4. Prayer or Connection with God: Strengthening Faith

For those who practice a faith tradition, prayer can be a central part of spiritual health. Prayer is more than a routine; it's a way to connect with God, seek guidance, and find comfort in times of uncertainty. Taking time each day to pray, whether in the morning, before meals, or before bed, allows you to connect with your faith and remember that you're not alone in your journey.

If prayer is part of your spiritual practice, make it a habit to pause and express gratitude, seek wisdom, or share your thoughts. If you don't practice prayer, you might find value in another form of spiritual connection, such as spending time in nature, practicing mindfulness, or simply sitting in silence to feel a sense of connection with something greater than yourself.

5. Journaling: A Tool for Reflection and Growth

Journaling is an excellent way to process thoughts, clarify values, and reflect on experiences. Setting aside a few minutes each day or week to write about your challenges, victories, and lessons learned can provide powerful insights. This practice not only helps you track your progress but also gives you a dedicated space to explore your emotions, dreams, and spiritual beliefs.

You might consider a structured journaling approach where you answer specific questions: "What am I grateful for today?" "What did I learn this week?" or "How can I live more fully aligned with my values?" Journaling can serve as a mirror, allowing you to see how your spiritual health influences your life and leadership. As you look back on your entries, you'll see patterns and insights that help you grow over time.

6. Mindful Walking or Nature Time: Connecting with the Present

Sometimes, the most spiritual experiences come from simply being present. Taking a walk outdoors, feeling the breeze, and noticing the beauty of nature can be a deeply grounding experience. If you're feeling stressed or overwhelmed, stepping outside for a mindful walk can help you reset and reconnect with yourself.

During a mindful walk, leave behind distractions and focus on the sights, sounds, and sensations around you. Feel the ground beneath your feet, listen to the rustle of leaves, and breathe in the fresh air. This practice not only calms the mind but also reminds you of the beauty and interconnectedness of life. For many leaders, time in nature serves as a reminder of their purpose, offering perspective and peace.

7. Acts of Service: Giving Back as a Spiritual Practice

Serving others can be one of the most fulfilling ways to nurture your spiritual health. When we focus on helping those around us—whether through mentorship, volunteering, or small acts of kindness—we tap into the part of ourselves that is deeply connected to others. Service reminds us that leadership isn't just about achieving our own goals; it's about lifting others and making a positive impact.

Consider incorporating acts of service into your life, both inside and outside of work. This might mean mentoring a colleague, volunteering for a cause you care about, or simply being a supportive friend. By prioritizing service, you create a ripple effect of positivity and inspiration, both for yourself and for those you lead.

8. Evening Reflection: Closing the Day with Gratitude and Intention

Just as morning reflection helps you start the day with clarity, an evening reflection allows you to end it with gratitude and peace. Taking a few moments before bed to reflect on the day's events can be a powerful way to wind down and connect with your spiritual health.

During your evening reflection, consider asking yourself, "What went well today?" "What am I thankful for?" and "What can I let go of to rest peacefully?" This habit not only helps you end the day on a positive note but also encourages restful sleep as you release any tension or worries that may be lingering. Over time, this habit strengthens your ability to live with intention and to appreciate each day fully.

Creating a Consistent Spiritual Routine

Building spiritual health isn't about adopting every single technique; it's about finding what resonates most with you and making it a consistent part of your life. A few well-chosen practices that truly connect with your values and beliefs will have a greater impact than trying to do it all. Start with one or two habits that feel meaningful, and incorporate them into your daily or weekly routine.

Remember, nurturing your spiritual health is a journey, not a destination. Some days, these practices will feel effortless and fulfilling; other days, they may feel like a challenge. Be patient with yourself and trust that each small effort is contributing to your growth. Over time, these spiritual habits become a source of strength, resilience, and peace that sustains you in your leadership and your life.

Spiritual health is not something separate from who you are as a leader—it's the foundation that allows you to lead with clarity, compassion, and courage. By prioritizing your spiritual well-being, you create a life that is balanced, purposeful, and deeply fulfilling, making you a stronger, more inspiring leader for those around you.

Chapter 3

Train Your Brain or Remain The Same

As female leaders, we often find ourselves juggling multiple responsibilities, making decisions under pressure, and facing challenges that test our resilience. The ability to stay focused, think clearly, and make decisions with confidence is vital to our success. But just like physical fitness, mental fitness is something we must actively work on and cultivate. It's not something that happens by accident. To lead effectively, we need to be intentional about training our brains, building mental toughness, and developing strategies that support our clarity and resilience.

Mental fitness is about more than just staying sharp or being able to focus. It's about managing stress, adapting to change, staying present, and maintaining a positive mindset in the face of adversity. In this chapter, we'll explore mental fitness practices that can enhance your decision-making, improve your problem-solving skills, and help you stay grounded in difficult situations. These practices are not just about reacting to stress—they're about building a mental foundation that empowers you to lead with confidence, clarity, and strength.

The Power of the Mind: Why Mental Fitness Matters

Your mind is one of your most powerful tools as a leader. It influences how you perceive the world, how you interact with others, and how you approach challenges. A well-trained mind allows you to think critically, solve problems, and make decisions that align with your values and goals. It also helps you navigate the emotional ups and downs of leadership, giving you the ability to stay calm and focused, even in high-pressure situations.

However, just like a muscle, your mind needs to be exercised regularly in order to stay sharp and resilient. Mental fitness isn't something you're born with—it's a skill that you can develop and strengthen over time. The stronger your mental fitness, the more effectively you'll be able to handle stress, adapt to change, and make decisions that move you toward your goals.

Building Mental Fitness: Key Practices for Strengthening Your Mind

Building mental fitness requires intentional practices that challenge your mind, help you build resilience, and keep you grounded. The following techniques are some of the most effective ways to train your brain for better decision-making and greater resilience:

1. Mindfulness: Being Present and Focused

Mindfulness is the practice of being fully present in the moment without judgment. In today's fast-paced world, it's easy to become distracted or overwhelmed by the constant flow of information and demands on our time. Mindfulness helps you clear the mental clutter and focus on the task at hand, which is essential for making clear, informed decisions.

To practice mindfulness, start by dedicating a few minutes each day to simply being present. Sit quietly, breathe deeply, and focus on the sensations in your body and the thoughts in your mind. You don't need to force your thoughts to stop—just observe them without judgment. This simple practice helps train your brain to stay focused and reduces mental distractions that can hinder your decision-making.

As you become more accustomed to mindfulness, you'll notice that it's easier to stay calm and clear-headed, even when faced with stressful situations. When you practice mindfulness regularly, you train your brain to stay in the present moment, which improves focus, clarity, and resilience.

2. Positive Self-Talk: Reframing Negative Thoughts

Your thoughts have a powerful influence on your emotions and actions. Negative self-talk can undermine your confidence, cause unnecessary stress, and cloud your judgment. On the other hand, positive self-talk can boost your resilience, help you stay optimistic, and enhance your decision-making skills.

To improve your mental fitness, begin to pay attention to the language you use with yourself. When you face a challenge or difficult decision, do you automatically think, "I can't do this," or "This is too hard"? If so, practice reframing these thoughts into something more positive: "I can handle this," or "This is an opportunity for growth." The more you replace negative thoughts with constructive, empowering ones, the more you'll build mental resilience and increase your ability to handle challenges with confidence.

Another powerful way to shift your mindset is by using affirmations. Choose a few positive statements that resonate with you, such as "I am a capable leader" or "I trust myself to make the right decisions." Repeat these affirmations daily to train your brain to focus on your strengths rather than your perceived weaknesses.

3. Visualization: Seeing Success Before It Happens

Visualization is a technique used by athletes, performers, and leaders to mentally rehearse success. By vividly imagining yourself succeeding in a particular situation, you program your mind to believe that success is possible. Visualization boosts confidence, strengthens resilience, and improves decision-making by reducing anxiety and clarifying your goals.

To practice visualization, find a quiet space and close your eyes. Imagine yourself in a situation where you need to make an important decision or overcome a challenge. Picture yourself handling the situation with calm, confidence, and clarity. See yourself making the right choice and achieving the desired outcome. The more vividly you visualize success, the more confident and prepared you will feel when the actual moment arrives.

Visualization works because it helps your brain practice and prepare for success, which reduces fear and self-doubt. It also activates the neural pathways associated with goal achievement, making it easier for your brain to recognize opportunities and take decisive action when the time comes.

4. Resilience Training: Bouncing Back from Adversity

Resilience is the ability to bounce back from setbacks, adapt to challenges, and keep moving forward, even when things don't go as planned. As a leader, resilience is crucial for navigating the inevitable obstacles and difficulties you'll face in your career. It's what allows you to stay focused, maintain your emotional balance, and make sound decisions during times of stress.

To build resilience, focus on developing a growth mindset. This means viewing challenges as opportunities to learn and grow rather than as threats. When you face a setback, ask yourself, "What can I learn from this experience?" "How can I grow from this?" By reframing challenges as learning opportunities, you train your brain to remain flexible, optimistic, and forward-focused.

Another key aspect of resilience is maintaining emotional balance. Practice stress-management techniques like deep breathing, exercise, or journaling to keep your emotions in check during high-pressure moments. By regularly managing your stress and practicing emotional regulation, you'll increase your ability to bounce back quickly from setbacks and make decisions that are aligned with your long-term goals.

5. Decision-Making Strategies: Making Clear Choices Under Pressure

As a leader, you're often required to make difficult decisions with limited information and under tight deadlines. Developing a mental framework for decision-making can help you make better choices, even in high-pressure situations.

One powerful strategy is to use the "pros and cons" method: list the potential benefits and drawbacks of each option and then weigh them based on their importance. This allows you to take a step back, assess the situation logically, and make a decision based on facts rather than emotions or pressure. Another useful method is to ask yourself, "What's the worst-case scenario?" By considering the possible consequences of your choices, you can make more informed decisions with greater confidence.

In addition, trust your intuition. As a leader, you have a wealth of experience and insight that can guide your decision-making. While it's important to analyze the facts, don't underestimate the value of your gut instincts. When you combine rational thinking with intuitive insight, you make decisions that are both logical and aligned with your deeper values.

Enhancing Your Mental Fitness: A Lifelong Practice

Building mental fitness is a lifelong practice. It's not something that happens overnight but rather a continuous process of training your brain to handle stress, make sound decisions, and stay resilient in the face of adversity. The more you practice mental fitness techniques, the stronger your mind will become. Over time, these habits will become second nature, and you'll find that your decision-making improves, your resilience strengthens, and your leadership becomes more focused and purposeful.

By prioritizing mental fitness, you'll not only become a better leader—you'll also be better equipped to live a balanced and fulfilling life. With a strong, resilient mind, you'll be able to face any challenge with confidence, make decisions with clarity, and lead others with strength and integrity.

Your mind is one of your greatest assets, and just like your body, it requires regular training and care. The practices outlined in this chapter will help you build a solid mental foundation that supports your leadership, decision-making, and resilience. By consistently nurturing your mental fitness, you can lead with confidence, clarity, and purpose—no matter what challenges lie ahead.

******

Cognitive Strategies to Maintain Mental Clarity and Focus

As leaders, our ability to think clearly, maintain focus, and make sharp, informed decisions is essential. Mental clarity and focus are foundational for effective leadership—they allow us to stay on track with our goals, lead with purpose, and respond to challenges with wisdom. But in the face of constant distractions, shifting priorities, and the pressure of daily responsibilities, maintaining mental clarity can feel like a constant battle.

The good news is that mental clarity and focus are not just traits you're born with—they can be developed and strengthened through intentional practices. Cognitive strategies are the mental tools and techniques that help you maintain focus, reduce mental fog, and improve your decision-making. In this section, we'll explore strategies that can help you clear away distractions, sharpen your concentration, and keep your mind focused on what truly matters.

1. The Power of Prioritization: Focusing on What Matters Most

One of the most effective strategies for maintaining mental clarity is learning how to prioritize. As a leader, you're often juggling many responsibilities at once, and it's easy to become overwhelmed by the sheer volume of tasks. The key to staying clear-headed is knowing where to direct your energy and attention. This begins with understanding your top priorities.

Start by identifying your most important goals—those that will have the greatest impact on your personal and professional growth. These are the tasks and projects that deserve your undivided attention. When you prioritize these, you'll naturally filter out distractions and avoid wasting energy on things that don't align with your bigger vision.

A simple technique for prioritization is the *Eisenhower Matrix*, which categorizes tasks based on urgency and importance. This matrix helps you distinguish between tasks that are truly critical and those that are simply urgent but not important. By focusing on what truly matters, you can clear the mental clutter and direct your energy where it will make the most impact.

Another way to prioritize effectively is by setting clear intentions for the day. At the beginning of each day, take a few minutes to reflect on what you want to accomplish. Writing down your top three priorities can help you stay focused and ensure that you don't get sidetracked by less important tasks.

2. Time Blocking: Creating Mental Space for Deep Work

Mental clarity is often compromised by the constant flow of tasks, meetings, emails, and messages. To protect your focus, you need to create time blocks in your schedule for uninterrupted work. Time blocking is a technique where you designate specific periods of time for certain tasks and activities, allowing you to immerse yourself fully in one thing at a time.

For example, you might block off two hours in the morning for focused work on a high-priority project, during which you'll avoid checking emails or answering calls. By giving yourself dedicated time to work without interruptions, you allow your brain to dive deep into the task at hand, which enhances both your focus and productivity.

Time blocking is particularly helpful for leaders because it encourages discipline and reduces the temptation to multitask, which often leads to mental fatigue and reduced clarity. When you know exactly when you'll focus on a particular task, you can be fully present and clear-headed during that time.

Another benefit of time blocking is that it allows you to balance different types of tasks—creative, strategic, administrative—throughout your day. Scheduling these tasks during times when you are naturally more alert and focused ensures that you're using your mental energy efficiently.

3. Single-Tasking: The Art of Focused Attention

Multitasking may seem like a necessary skill in today's fast-paced world, but it often leads to reduced focus, increased stress, and mental exhaustion. In fact, studies show that multitasking can impair cognitive performance, as the brain has to constantly switch between tasks, leading to loss of focus and productivity.

Instead, consider embracing the art of single-tasking or focusing on one task at a time. When you focus solely on one thing, you are able to give it your full attention and energy, which not only improves the quality of your work but also helps maintain mental clarity.

To practice single-tasking, eliminate distractions. Turn off notifications, close unnecessary tabs on your computer, and set a timer for a specific amount of time to work on a single task. The Pomodoro Technique is one approach to this, where you work for 25-minute intervals followed by a short break. These intervals allow your brain to remain engaged without feeling overloaded, helping you sustain focus and mental clarity throughout the day.

In addition to helping you stay focused, single-tasking improves decision-making because it allows you to give more thought to each task, making it easier to assess what is important and what needs further attention.

4. Mental Detachment: Taking Breaks to Recharge

Sometimes, the best way to maintain mental clarity is to step away from the task at hand. Mental fatigue and stress build up when we don't give ourselves adequate breaks. Constantly pushing through without rest can lead to burnout, clouded judgment, and poor decision-making.

Taking regular breaks throughout the day is essential for maintaining mental clarity. These breaks don't have to be long, but they should allow your brain to reset and recharge. Research shows that taking breaks can actually improve focus and productivity, as it gives your brain a chance to process information and recover from cognitive overload.

During your breaks, engage in activities that help you relax and refocus—whether it's going for a short walk, practicing deep breathing, or simply closing your eyes for a few minutes of quiet time. You can also consider stepping outside for fresh air or having a brief conversation with a colleague to refresh your mind. The key is to detach mentally from the work at hand so that when you return, you're able to engage with it more clearly and with renewed energy.

5. Mindful Breathing: Calming the Mind and Reducing Stress

When you're feeling overwhelmed or stressed, your mental clarity can quickly diminish. Mindful breathing is a simple but effective cognitive strategy to calm the mind and bring clarity back. Taking a few minutes to focus on your breath can lower stress levels, improve focus, and help clear mental fog.

A simple breathing technique you can try is the 4-7-8 method: inhale for four seconds, hold your breath for seven seconds, and exhale for eight seconds. This technique helps activate your parasympathetic nervous system, which relaxes your body and mind, reducing stress and improving focus.

You can also practice deep belly breathing, where you focus on filling your lungs with air and expanding your diaphragm, rather than shallow chest breathing. This type of breathing promotes relaxation and helps clear your mind of distractions, enabling you to focus more clearly on the task at hand.

In moments of stress or indecision, a few minutes of mindful breathing can help you reset, reducing anxiety and allowing you to approach challenges with a calm and focused mind.

6. Cognitive Reframing: Shifting Perspectives to Enhance Problem-Solving

As a leader, you'll often face complex problems and difficult decisions. Cognitive reframing is a mental technique that allows you to shift your perspective and look at a situation from a new angle. By reframing, you can reduce stress, increase mental clarity, and make more effective decisions.

When faced with a challenging situation, ask yourself questions like: "What opportunities are there in this challenge?" "What can I learn from this situation?" or "How can I approach this differently to achieve a better outcome?" This reframing process helps you break free from negative thought patterns and opens up new solutions, leading to clearer thinking and better decision-making.

Reframing also helps you manage uncertainty by shifting your focus away from the problem and toward the possibilities. By training your brain to reframe challenges positively, you'll develop a clearer, more solution-oriented mindset that enhances your ability to lead effectively.

Maintaining Mental Clarity: A Lifelong Practice

Developing and maintaining mental clarity is not a one-time effort—it's a lifelong practice. The strategies outlined in this chapter are tools that, when practiced consistently, will help you stay focused, make better decisions, and lead with greater resilience. By prioritizing your mental fitness, you are building a strong foundation for yourself and your leadership, enabling you to navigate the complexities of life and work with clarity, purpose, and strength.

Mental clarity and focus are vital to success, not just in leadership but in every aspect of life. By incorporating these cognitive strategies into your routine, you'll be able to make decisions with confidence, stay grounded under pressure, and maintain the mental energy needed to lead effectively. Over time, these practices will become second nature, allowing you to lead with clarity and focus, even in the midst of chaos.

Chapter 4

Your Body is a Temple

As leaders, we often find ourselves at the helm of responsibility, making decisions, managing teams, and navigating challenges. But no matter how brilliant our minds or how committed we are to our work, there is one thing that we can never afford to overlook: the health of our bodies. Our bodies are the vessels that carry us through every task, every meeting, every conversation. They are the foundation of our stamina, energy, and resilience as leaders. When we neglect our physical health, we are essentially compromising our ability to lead with full strength and presence.

The saying "Your body is a temple" holds a powerful truth. It reminds us that we must take care of ourselves if we are to show up fully for others. In leadership, physical health is not a luxury or afterthought; it is an essential part of our ability to perform at our best, to inspire those around us, and to navigate the long hours, the stressful days, and the constant demands of leadership. This chapter will explore why physical health is so crucial for leadership stamina and presence and provide practical insights on how to nurture your body to unlock your fullest potential.

The Link Between Physical Health and Leadership Stamina

As a leader, your ability to maintain stamina—both mentally and physically—is essential to your success. Leadership demands a lot from us: long hours, high expectations, and constant decision-making. If we don't have the energy to keep up, our ability to lead diminishes. We might start to feel sluggish, tired, or easily overwhelmed, which affects not only our performance but also our interactions with those we lead.

Physical health directly impacts our stamina. When our bodies are strong, well-nourished, and rested, we have the energy to sustain us throughout the day. A healthy body gives us the resilience to keep going, even when the pressure is high. You've likely experienced this yourself—on days when you've eaten well, slept enough, and exercised, you can feel the difference in your energy levels. You're more alert, more present, and more able to handle whatever comes your way. On the flip side, when you're not taking care of your body, everything feels harder. Your energy wanes, and your decision-making becomes clouded.

That's why maintaining physical health isn't just about looking good; it's about ensuring that your body has the strength and stamina to carry you through the demands of leadership. When you take care of your body, you are not only improving your physical appearance but also setting yourself up for success in every aspect of your leadership journey.

The Power of Exercise: Strengthening the Body and Mind

Exercise is one of the most powerful tools for building both physical health and leadership stamina. It not only strengthens the body but also enhances mental clarity, emotional regulation, and resilience. When we exercise, our bodies release endorphins, which are natural mood boosters. This can help reduce stress and anxiety, making it easier to navigate the highs and lows of leadership.

But, the benefits of exercise go beyond mood and stress management. Regular physical activity improves cardiovascular health, boosts immune function, and increases energy levels—critical factors for maintaining the stamina needed for leadership. It also improves cognitive function, enhancing our ability to focus, think critically, and make sound decisions.

One of the most powerful things about exercise is that it doesn't have to be intense or time-consuming to be effective. Whether it's a 30-minute walk, a yoga session, or a quick workout in the gym, consistency is key. Find an exercise routine that works for you and make it a regular part of your schedule. The important thing is to move your body regularly and make time for physical activity, no matter how busy life gets.

In addition to the physical benefits, exercise provides a mental reset. It's a time to clear your head, focus on your body, and take a break from the mental demands of leadership. This is why many successful leaders prioritize exercise—they know that it not only keeps them healthy but also sharpens their minds and increases their ability to lead effectively.

Nutrition: Fueling the Body for Peak Performance

Just as exercise strengthens the body, proper nutrition fuels it. What you eat directly impacts how you feel and perform. In leadership, we need sustained energy throughout the day to make decisions, solve problems, and stay present for our teams. If we're eating foods that cause energy crashes or leave us feeling sluggish, we're not setting ourselves up for success.

Fueling your body with nutritious foods provides the energy you need to thrive. A diet rich in whole foods—such as vegetables, fruits, lean proteins, and healthy fats—supports your physical health and cognitive function. Avoiding processed foods and excess sugar can help maintain steady energy levels and prevent the mid-afternoon slumps that many of us experience.

In addition to providing energy, the right nutrition helps maintain your immune system, regulate your hormones, and promote mental clarity. It's also important to stay hydrated throughout the day, as dehydration can lead to fatigue, headaches, and difficulty focusing. Drinking water regularly and consuming foods with high water content (like fruits and vegetables) will help you stay energized and focused.

As a leader, you are the model for those around you. When you prioritize healthy eating, you not only improve your own performance but also encourage those you lead to do the same. A leader who makes conscious choices about their health sets an example of discipline, intentionality, and self-care.

Sleep: The Foundation of Rest and Recovery

It's impossible to overstate the importance of sleep in maintaining physical health and leadership stamina. Sleep is the time when our bodies and minds recover, regenerate, and recharge. Without adequate sleep, our bodies become fatigued, our cognitive function declines, and our ability to make clear decisions diminishes.

Good quality sleep is the foundation of physical health. It's when your body repairs itself, strengthens your immune system, and consolidates memories. Without it, we're simply running on empty, and it becomes harder to maintain focus, energy, and resilience. As leaders, we often prioritize work over rest, pushing ourselves to stay up late or wake up early to get more done. But this only leads to burnout and diminished performance in the long run.

To maintain leadership stamina, it's essential to prioritize sleep as part of your daily routine. Aim for 7-9 hours of quality sleep each night. Create a bedtime routine that helps signal to your body that it's time to wind down—this might include turning off electronic devices an hour before bed, reading a book, or practicing relaxation techniques like deep breathing or meditation.

Quality sleep improves mental clarity, decision-making, and emotional regulation, which are crucial for leading with presence and purpose. Leaders who value sleep are better equipped to handle the pressures of their roles and lead with the energy and focus their teams need.

The Role of Stress Management: Keeping the Body in Balance

As leaders, stress is inevitable. We face high-stakes decisions, navigate conflicts, and work long hours to achieve our goals. But when stress is left unchecked, it can take a toll on both our physical and mental health. Chronic stress can lead to a weakened immune system, high blood pressure, and fatigue. It also affects our ability to think clearly, make decisions, and respond with resilience.

That's why stress management is a critical aspect of physical health. By managing stress effectively, we can protect our bodies from the negative effects of long-term stress and maintain the energy we need to lead. One of the most effective stress-management strategies is regular physical activity. Exercise helps release built-up tension and promotes relaxation. In addition, practices like meditation, mindfulness, or even spending time outdoors can help reduce stress and promote a sense of balance.

It's also important to recognize when stress is becoming overwhelming and take the necessary steps to address it. Whether it's through delegating tasks, setting boundaries, or taking time off, it's essential to listen to your body and give yourself the rest and recovery you need.

Leadership Presence: How Physical Health Impacts How You Show Up

As leaders, our presence matters. The way we show up—both physically and emotionally—affects how others perceive us and how they respond to our leadership. A leader who is physically healthy radiates energy, confidence, and focus, which inspires others to perform at their best.

Physical health directly impacts our leadership presence. When we feel strong, energized, and well-rested, we project confidence and clarity. We're able to engage fully in conversations, make decisions with conviction, and lead with a sense of purpose. On the other hand, when we're exhausted, stressed, or physically unwell, our energy and presence can suffer, and our ability to lead with impact is diminished.

By prioritizing physical health, we are not only taking care of ourselves but also enhancing our leadership presence. When we take care of our bodies, we create the strength and vitality we need to lead with confidence, resilience, and authenticity.

Your Body is Your Foundation for Leadership Success

Your physical health is the foundation upon which everything else is built—your stamina, your decision-making, your ability to lead with presence, and your capacity to inspire those around you. By prioritizing your body—through regular exercise, proper nutrition, quality sleep, and effective stress management—you create a strong, resilient foundation that enables you to lead with energy, focus, and purpose.

Remember, as a leader, you set the tone for those around you. When you take care of your body, you not only improve your own performance but also model healthy behaviors for those you lead. Your body is a temple—treat it with the care, respect, and attention it deserves, and you'll find that you have the stamina and presence to lead with strength, resilience, and impact.

******

Practical Tips for Fitness, Nutrition, and Work-Life Balance

As leaders, our ability to perform at our highest level is deeply connected to the state of our bodies. When we are physically fit, well-nourished, and able to maintain balance in our lives, we are more equipped to lead with energy, clarity, and purpose. Yet, in the whirlwind of leadership responsibilities, it can be all too easy to overlook the importance of taking care of ourselves. This section offers practical, actionable tips for maintaining your fitness, nourishing your body, and achieving a healthy work-life balance—so you can be the leader you're meant to be.

Fitness: Making Movement Part of Your Routine

Exercise is not just about looking good or staying healthy—it's an investment in your leadership. Regular physical activity boosts your energy, enhances your mood, sharpens your focus, and helps you manage stress. Whether you're a seasoned athlete or someone just starting on their fitness journey, incorporating movement into your daily routine is essential for maintaining leadership stamina and presence.

Here are some practical fitness tips that can easily be incorporated into your busy schedule:

1. **Start Small and Build Consistency**: The key to fitness is consistency, not intensity. If you're new to regular exercise, start with short, manageable workouts. Even 20-30 minutes a day can make a huge difference in your energy levels and overall health. You can gradually increase the duration or intensity as your body adapts.

2. **Incorporate Movement Into Your Day**: If you're pressed for time, look for opportunities to move throughout the day. Take the stairs instead of the elevator, walk or bike to meetings if possible, or schedule short "movement breaks" between tasks. Even a quick 5-minute stretch or walk can re-energize you and sharpen your focus.

3. **Mix It Up**: To avoid burnout or boredom, vary your workout routine. Include a mix of strength training, cardio, flexibility, and mobility exercises to keep things interesting and target different areas of your body. Find something you enjoy—whether it's yoga, swimming, running, or a dance class—so that fitness doesn't feel like a chore but something you look forward to.

4. **Prioritize Rest and Recovery**: Just as important as regular exercise is giving your body the rest it needs. Overworking your body without adequate recovery can lead to burnout or injury. Make sure to get enough sleep, incorporate rest days into your fitness routine, and practice relaxation techniques like stretching or meditation to allow your body to recover.

5. **Set Realistic Fitness Goals**: Setting goals can help keep you motivated, but make sure they're realistic. Whether it's increasing your endurance, lifting heavier weights, or improving your flexibility, setting small, achievable goals will give you a sense of accomplishment and keep you on track.

Nutrition: Fueling Your Body for Peak Performance

What we eat has a profound effect on our energy levels, focus, and overall health. As leaders, we need to fuel our bodies with the right nutrients to maintain peak performance throughout the day. Proper nutrition provides the energy needed for decision-making, problem-solving, and maintaining a positive, productive attitude.

Here are some practical nutrition tips that will support your leadership and overall well-being:

1. **Focus on Whole, Nutrient-Dense Foods**: A balanced diet rich in whole, unprocessed foods is the foundation for good health. Prioritize vegetables, fruits, lean proteins (like chicken, fish, tofu, and legumes), whole grains (like brown rice, quinoa, and oats), and healthy fats (such as avocado, nuts, and olive oil). These foods provide the nutrients your body needs to stay energized, focused, and healthy.

2. **Eat Regular, Balanced Meals**: To maintain steady energy levels, avoid skipping meals or relying on sugary snacks. Instead, aim to eat balanced meals every 3-4 hours. Include a combination of protein, healthy fats, and fiber in each meal to stabilize your blood sugar and keep you feeling full and focused. For example, a meal with grilled salmon, quinoa, and a side of roasted vegetables will provide lasting energy without a sugar crash.

3. **Stay Hydrated**: Hydration is critical for mental clarity, focus, and energy. Dehydration can lead to fatigue, headaches, and difficulty concentrating, so make sure you're drinking enough water throughout the day. A good rule of thumb is to aim for half your

body weight in ounces of water per day. If you drink coffee or tea, be sure to balance it with extra water to counteract dehydration.

4. **Limit Processed Foods and Sugary Snacks**: While it's tempting to grab a quick snack or drink when you're busy, processed foods and sugary snacks can cause energy spikes followed by crashes, which ultimately affect your productivity. Instead, choose whole-food snacks like nuts, fruit, yogurt, or vegetables with hummus to keep your energy levels steady throughout the day.

5. **Plan Ahead and Prepare Meals**: In our fast-paced lives, it's easy to resort to unhealthy convenience foods when we're in a hurry. To make healthier eating easier, plan and prepare your meals ahead of time. Batch-cooking healthy meals on the weekend or using a slow cooker can save time and ensure you have nutritious meals ready to go when you need them.

6. **Mindful Eating**: Eating on the go or while distracted can lead to overeating or poor digestion. Practice mindful eating by slowing down, chewing your food properly, and paying attention to how you feel before, during, and after meals. This will not only improve digestion but also help you tune in to your body's hunger and fullness signals.

Work-Life Balance: Finding Harmony Between Leadership and Life

Maintaining a healthy work-life balance is perhaps one of the most challenging aspects of leadership. With all the demands on our time, it's easy to let work take over and neglect other important areas of our lives. However, if we don't make time for rest, relaxation, and self-care, we risk burnout, which ultimately affects our performance as leaders.

Achieving work-life balance doesn't mean giving up on your career goals or personal aspirations; it's about finding harmony and ensuring that both your professional and personal life are aligned with your values and priorities.

Here are some practical tips to help you maintain balance:

1. **Set Boundaries and Prioritize Your Time**: As a leader, you may feel like you're constantly needed or expected to be available. While it's important to be responsive to your team, it's equally important to set boundaries. Establish clear work hours and make time for your personal life—whether it's spending time with family, pursuing hobbies, or simply resting. Setting boundaries will help prevent burnout and ensure you're fully present when you are working or with loved ones.

2. **Learn to Delegate**: One of the most effective ways to balance work and life is by delegating tasks. You don't have to do everything yourself. Trust your team to handle certain responsibilities, and empower them to take ownership of projects. Delegating allows you to focus on the bigger picture and the areas where your leadership is most needed.

3. **Schedule Downtime and Rest**: Just as you schedule meetings and work-related tasks, make sure to schedule downtime in your calendar. This might include taking a walk, reading a book, or simply taking a few minutes to breathe deeply and reset. Regular rest and recovery are essential for maintaining mental and physical health, so don't feel guilty for taking breaks or stepping away from work.

4. **Make Time for What You Love**: A fulfilling life outside of work is key to maintaining balance. Whether it's spending time with loved ones, traveling, practicing a hobby, or simply relaxing, make sure you're carving out time to do the things that bring you joy and recharge your energy. A fulfilling personal life enhances your overall well-being and gives you the strength to show up fully as a leader.

5. **Practice Self-Compassion**: Achieving work-life balance is not about perfection. There will be times when work demands more of

your time and times when your personal life takes priority. The key is to be compassionate with yourself and understand that balance is dynamic and ever-changing. Don't beat yourself up when things don't go as planned—simply adjust and move forward.

Prioritize Your Health, Lead with Strength

As a leader, your body is the vessel through which you carry out your vision and execute your goals. Maintaining physical health is not a luxury; it's a necessity for sustaining the stamina, energy, and presence required to lead effectively. By incorporating regular exercise, mindful nutrition, and practices that support work-life balance, you create a strong foundation for both personal and professional success.

When you take care of your body, you show up as your best self. You become more resilient in the face of challenges, more focused in your decision-making, and more present for those you lead. Leadership isn't just about making decisions or managing tasks—it's about showing up fully in every moment. And that starts with taking care of the one thing that supports everything else: your body.

Make your health a priority, and you'll find that not only will you lead better, but you'll also live better, with energy, clarity, and balance.

Chapter 5

Let's Sum It Up

As we've journeyed through this book, we've explored how mastering your health is one of the most important pillars of leadership. From understanding the interconnectedness of physical, mental, and spiritual health to building practices that nurture each of these dimensions, you've been introduced to powerful strategies for elevating your well-being. Now, it's time to recap the key health strategies that will empower you to lead with strength, resilience, and clarity. These aren't just tips—they're life-changing habits that, when integrated into your daily routine, can transform the way you show up for yourself and for others.

Leadership is demanding. It requires stamina, focus, and the ability to handle stress and challenges with grace. But these qualities don't just emerge on their own. They come from a place of balance and well-being. And just as you wouldn't expect a car to run efficiently without proper fuel, you can't expect to lead effectively without nurturing your own health.

So, let's take a moment to reflect on the health strategies we've covered in the previous chapters and see how each one contributes to your leadership potential.

1. Three-Dimensional Health: Balancing Body, Mind, and Spirit

The foundation of your health as a leader begins with the recognition that you are a multi-dimensional being. Your physical, mental, and spiritual health are deeply interconnected, and it's only when all three are nurtured that you can achieve true balance and vitality.

Physical health fuels your energy, stamina, and resilience. By exercising regularly, eating a nutritious diet, and prioritizing rest, you ensure your body has the strength to carry you through the demands of leadership.

Mental health sharpens your decision-making, focus, and emotional resilience. Practices like mindfulness, positive self-talk, and mental training techniques help you stay clear-headed under pressure, making it easier to solve problems, think strategically, and lead with clarity.

Spiritual health is the grounding force that provides you with a sense of purpose and direction. By staying connected to your values, purpose, and faith, you tap into a source of strength that enables you to lead with integrity, compassion, and resilience.

The key takeaway here is that when you care for your whole self—physically, mentally, and spiritually—you create a balanced foundation for effective leadership. Don't neglect one aspect for the sake of another. When all three dimensions are aligned, you'll lead with greater clarity, presence, and confidence.

2. Physical Health: The Power of Stamina and Presence

Your body is the vehicle that carries you through each day of leadership. Without physical health, your energy will be drained, your mind will be foggy, and your presence will wane. To lead effectively, you need to have the stamina to sustain you through the highs and lows of leadership.

In this chapter, we covered the importance of **exercise**, **nutrition**, and **sleep** in maintaining leadership stamina. Regular physical activity boosts your energy levels, enhances your cognitive function, and builds resilience to stress. Eating a balanced diet supports your physical and mental well-being, helping you stay sharp and focused throughout the day. And quality sleep is the bedrock of both physical and mental health—it's essential for recovery, energy, and decision-making.

You don't need to be a fitness expert or follow an extreme diet to benefit from these practices. The key is consistency. Make small, sustainable changes that fit your lifestyle, and commit to taking care of your body every day. Whether it's a walk after lunch, a simple morning stretch, or a healthier meal choice, these actions add up over time and make a world of difference in how you show up as a leader.

3. Mental Fitness: Training the Brain for Clarity and Resilience

Just as we exercise our bodies to build strength, we must also train our minds to build resilience and mental clarity. Mental fitness involves developing the skills and habits that allow you to handle stress, make sound decisions, and maintain focus under pressure.

We explored several strategies for improving mental fitness, including **mindfulness**, **positive self-talk**, and **visualization**. By practicing mindfulness, you train your brain to stay present, reducing distractions and improving focus. Positive self-talk helps you overcome limiting beliefs and empowers you to lead with confidence. And visualization techniques allow you to mentally rehearse success, which boosts your performance and enhances your ability to make decisions with clarity.

Mental fitness is about more than just reacting to stress—it's about proactively building mental resilience so you can bounce back from setbacks and continue leading with confidence. The stronger your mental fitness, the more equipped you'll be to handle challenges, think clearly, and make decisions that align with your vision.

4. Spiritual Health: Leading with Purpose and Integrity

Spiritual health is the cornerstone of authentic leadership. It's what gives you the strength and direction to navigate the challenges of leadership with purpose, compassion, and resilience. Your spiritual well-being doesn't have to be tied to a specific religion or practice. It's about staying connected to your core values, your higher purpose, and the deeper meaning behind your work.

In this chapter, we discussed the importance of nurturing your spiritual health through practices like **prayer**, **meditation**, and **journaling**. These practices help you stay grounded and focused on what truly matters. By regularly reflecting on your values and your purpose, you ensure that your leadership is aligned with your deeper vision rather than being driven solely by external pressures.

Spiritual health also plays a critical role in your resilience. When you face challenges or setbacks, it's your connection to something greater than yourself that helps you stay centered and strong. A spiritually grounded leader is one who leads with integrity, authenticity, and compassion—qualities that inspire trust and loyalty in others.

5. Building Consistency: Small Habits, Big Results

As we've seen throughout this book, the key to mastering health as a leader isn't about drastic changes or quick fixes—it's about building **small, sustainable habits** that create long-term results. Consistency is everything. It's not about being perfect every day; it's about showing up for yourself consistently, even on the hard days.

Whether it's taking ten minutes for mindfulness, going for a walk, eating a healthy meal, or getting enough sleep, each small action you take adds up over time. These habits compound and lead to bigger changes in your overall health, well-being, and leadership presence.

The best part? When you start prioritizing your health in small ways, the positive effects spill over into every area of your life. You'll feel more energized, more focused, and more confident in your leadership. And as you continue to lead with strength and clarity, you'll inspire those around you to do the same.

6. Creating a Sustainable Health Routine

The final strategy is about creating a **sustainable health routine**—one that fits your lifestyle, your goals, and your commitments. A sustainable routine isn't about trying to do everything at once or following a rigid, unrealistic plan. It's about setting manageable goals and making choices that are aligned with your vision for health and leadership.

Start by identifying the habits that work best for you and build them into your daily or weekly routine. Focus on the practices that resonate with you—whether it's a morning workout, a gratitude journal, or a regular meditation practice. Then, make these habits non-negotiable. The more consistent you are, the more ingrained these practices will become, and the more they will support your health and leadership in the long term.

Remember, the journey to health and well-being is ongoing. It's not about perfection—it's about progress. The goal is to continue evolving and growing as a leader by prioritizing your physical, mental, and spiritual health every day.

Leading from a Place of Strength

In closing, I want to remind you that as a leader, you are the most important asset in your organization. You cannot lead others effectively if you are neglecting your own well-being. By investing in your health—physically, mentally, and spiritually—you are creating the foundation for sustained leadership success. You are setting yourself up to lead with energy, clarity, and resilience, inspiring those around you to do the same.

The health strategies we've discussed throughout this book are not just tips or tricks—they are the building blocks of a leadership journey that is grounded in balance, authenticity, and purpose. When you nurture your health, you create the stamina, resilience, and presence that are essential for leading with impact.

Take these strategies and make them your own. Start small, stay consistent, and remember that every step you take toward improving your health is a step toward becoming the leader you were meant to be. Your body, mind, and spirit are your greatest assets—treat them with the care and respect they deserve, and you'll unlock your fullest potential as a leader.

******

Actionable Steps to Start Improving Health Immediately

Now that we've explored the essential strategies for mastering health in leadership, it's time to take action. Understanding the importance of physical, mental, and spiritual health is one thing, but the real transformation happens when we put these insights into practice. The key to lasting change is starting small and making intentional choices that build momentum over time. In this section, we'll walk through actionable steps you can begin today to start improving your health immediately. These are simple, practical habits that don't require drastic changes or complex systems—just a commitment to showing up for yourself.

The beauty of these steps is that you don't need to wait for the "perfect time" to start. You don't need to overhaul your entire lifestyle overnight. You can begin making improvements right now—today—and start seeing the benefits almost immediately. Whether you're focusing on physical fitness, mental clarity, or spiritual well-being, each small step you take will build on the last, creating lasting transformation over time.

1. Start Your Day with Intention: Morning Rituals for Success

The way you start your day sets the tone for everything that follows. A morning ritual is one of the most powerful ways to begin each day with purpose, focus, and clarity. When you take the time to care for yourself in the morning, you create a foundation of well-being that will carry you through the day.

Action Step:

a simple routine that nurtures your body, mind, and spirit. This might include:

- **Physical**: A few minutes of stretching or a light exercise routine to wake up your body and get your blood flowing.

- **Mental**: A few minutes of mindfulness or journaling. Reflect on your intentions for the day, write down your top three priorities, or practice positive affirmations.

- **Spiritual**: A moment of gratitude or prayer. Reflect on the things you're thankful for or connect with your spiritual beliefs to ground yourself before diving into the day.

Starting your day with intention will help you set a positive tone and bring focus to your day. By creating a morning routine that addresses your health on all levels—physical, mental, and spiritual—you are preparing yourself to face whatever challenges come your way.

2. Move Your Body: Prioritize Physical Activity

Exercise is one of the most effective ways to boost both your physical and mental health. It doesn't have to be a long or intense workout, but making movement a non-negotiable part of your routine will pay off in increased energy, better mood, and improved focus.

Action Step:

Commit to moving your body for at least 20 minutes a day. Choose something you enjoy—whether it's walking, yoga, dancing, or strength training. The goal is not to push yourself to exhaustion but to make physical activity a regular habit. Even small bursts of exercise, such as a walk around the block during lunch or a short stretching session in the morning, can have a huge impact on your overall health.

To make it stick, try scheduling your workouts like appointments in your calendar. Treat them with the same importance as a meeting or a deadline. When you prioritize physical activity, you are investing in the energy and resilience needed to lead effectively.

3. Eat for Energy: Nourish Your Body with Whole Foods

What you put into your body directly affects how you feel and perform. When we eat processed foods, sugary snacks, or junk food, we often experience energy crashes, mood swings, and difficulty focusing. On the other hand, nourishing your body with whole, nutrient-dense foods provides sustained energy and supports mental clarity.

Action Step:

Start by making small, sustainable changes to your diet. Begin by focusing on **whole, unprocessed foods**: fruits, vegetables, lean proteins, healthy fats, and whole grains. Aim to include a variety of colors and textures on your plate, as a diverse diet ensures you're getting a range of nutrients.

- **Make one healthy swap** today: Choose water over soda, or add a serving of vegetables to your lunch.

- **Plan your meals ahead of time** so you're not tempted by unhealthy options when you're busy or stressed.

You don't have to overhaul your entire diet at once. Begin with one healthy choice, and over time, these choices will become habits. When you fuel your body with the right nutrients, you'll experience better focus, higher energy levels, and improved decision-making.

4. Prioritize Sleep: Commit to Rest and Recovery

Quality sleep is the cornerstone of good health. Without enough rest, your mind and body cannot function at their best. Sleep is essential for recovery, cognitive function, emotional regulation, and overall well-being. Leaders who prioritize sleep are better able to handle stress, make clear decisions, and show up with the energy and presence their teams need.

Action Step:

Commit to getting 7-9 hours of sleep each night. To improve your sleep quality, try these tips:

- **Create a bedtime routine**: Set a time to wind down each night. This could involve reading, taking a warm bath, or practicing deep breathing.

- **Limit screen time**: Avoid screens (phones, computers, TVs) at least 30 minutes before bed, as the blue light can interfere with your body's production of melatonin, the hormone that helps you sleep.

- **Establish a consistent sleep schedule**: Try to go to bed and wake up at the same time every day, even on weekends. This helps regulate your internal clock and improves sleep quality over time.

Sleep is not a luxury—it's a necessity for leadership. When you prioritize rest, you set yourself up for a productive and focused day ahead.

5. Practice Stress Management: Stay Calm Under Pressure

Stress is inevitable, but how we manage it is key to our health and leadership effectiveness. Chronic stress can lead to burnout, fatigue, and poor decision-making. By developing healthy coping strategies, you can reduce the impact of stress on your body and mind.

Action Step:

Incorporate stress management practices into your daily routine. Here are a few simple techniques to try:

- **Deep breathing**: Take a few minutes each day to practice deep breathing exercises. Inhale for four seconds, hold for seven, and exhale for eight. This helps activate your parasympathetic nervous system, which calms your body and reduces stress.

- **Mindfulness**: Practice being present in the moment. If you feel overwhelmed, pause, take a few deep breaths, and focus on what's happening around you. This can help reduce feelings of stress and anxiety.

- **Take breaks**: Schedule time for short breaks throughout the day, especially when you're feeling stressed. Step outside for a walk, take a few minutes to stretch, or do something relaxing to reset your mind.

By developing these stress management practices, you'll be better equipped to handle challenges, maintain mental clarity, and lead with resilience.

6. Create Boundaries: Protect Your Time and Energy

As a leader, you are constantly pulled in many directions, which can leave you feeling drained. Setting boundaries is essential for maintaining your health and ensuring you have the energy to lead effectively. Boundaries allow you to protect your time, your mental space, and your personal well-being.

Action Step:

Start setting clear boundaries around your time and energy. Here's how you can do it:

- **Learn to say no**: Recognize that you can't do everything. Saying no to requests that don't align with your priorities is an act of self-respect and ensures you have the time and energy to focus on what matters most.

- **Designate work and personal time**: Set clear boundaries between work and personal life. When you're off the clock, disconnect from work emails and messages so you can fully recharge.

- **Create quiet time for yourself**: Set aside time each day to be alone, whether it's for reflection, reading, or just resting. This quiet time will help you reset and maintain balance.

Boundaries are not selfish—they're essential for maintaining your health and your ability to lead with presence and energy.

7. Stay Hydrated: Drink More Water

Staying hydrated is one of the simplest ways to support your physical health and mental clarity. Dehydration can lead to fatigue, headaches, and difficulty focusing, which can hinder your ability to perform at your best.

Action Step:

Make it a habit to drink water throughout the day. Aim for at least 8 cups (64 ounces) of water daily, and more if you're exercising or in a hot climate. Carry a water bottle with you so that you can sip water regularly, especially during meetings or while working.

Staying hydrated not only supports your physical health but also enhances your cognitive function and energy levels, making it easier to stay focused and clear-headed.

Start Today: Small Steps, Big Impact

Improving your health doesn't require a complete overhaul of your life—it's about making small, intentional changes that add up over time. By taking action today and committing to these simple steps, you are creating a strong foundation for sustained leadership success.

Remember, health is not just about what you do today—it's about what you commit to doing consistently. Start small, stay focused, and give yourself grace as you build new habits. Each small step you take today will pay off in greater energy, mental clarity, and resilience tomorrow. Take control of your health, and you'll be amazed at the transformation it brings to your leadership and your life.

Part II
Master Your LifeBottom of Form

Chapter 6

The Power in Subtraction

As leaders, we often believe that success comes from doing more—more work, more meetings, more commitments, more strategies. But what if I told you that true leadership success doesn't come from adding more to your life but from subtracting what's unnecessary? We're so often caught in the hustle of trying to do it all, thinking that more activity means more productivity, more impact, and more progress. Yet, in reality, it's the opposite. In order to create space for what truly matters, we must simplify our lives. We must let go of the clutter—both physical and mental—that distracts us from our purpose and steals our energy.

In this chapter, we'll explore the concept of *subtraction*—not as a limitation but as a powerful tool to enhance clarity, focus, and effectiveness. By removing distractions, excess commitments, and unnecessary stressors, we free up time and mental energy to focus on the things that truly matter. The result is not just a less chaotic life but a more intentional, purpose-driven one. Simplification is not about doing less for the sake of doing less. It's about making room for more of what truly serves you and your leadership journey.

The Myth of "More": Why Doing Less is Often the Key to Doing More

In today's world, we are often conditioned to believe that success means having more: more clients, more projects, more followers, more responsibilities. But as you've likely experienced, having more can quickly become overwhelming. More leads to distractions, burnout, and a lack of focus. It's easy to think that success is defined by the number of things we're involved in, but this mindset is counterproductive. When you are stretched too thin, you end up giving less of yourself to everything you do, which dilutes the quality of your work, your leadership, and your personal life.

The key to sustainable leadership is not in adding more to your plate but in *subtraction*. It's about focusing on the essential and eliminating what doesn't serve your bigger goals. When we clear away the clutter—whether it's physical, mental, or emotional—we can focus on what truly matters. This is the power of subtraction.

As a leader, you need to be ruthless about your time, energy, and focus. You need to ask yourself: What truly moves the needle forward? What commitments and activities are draining my energy or distracting me from my vision? What can I eliminate or delegate to create more space for what matters?

Simplifying Your Schedule: How to Prioritize What Matters

One of the most effective ways to simplify your life is by simplifying your schedule. Many of us are constantly running from one meeting to the next, feeling as though we must be in constant motion to be productive. But in reality, not every meeting, task, or event is essential. In fact, much of what fills our calendars doesn't move us closer to our goals; it simply fills the space.

Start by reviewing your schedule. How many meetings do you attend each week that could be streamlined, delegated, or eliminated altogether? How much time are you spending on tasks that don't directly align with your leadership goals? One simple way to simplify your schedule is to practice the 80/20 rule—the Pareto Principle. This rule suggests that 80% of your results come from 20% of your efforts. Take a closer look at your calendar and identify which tasks and commitments are giving you the highest return on investment. Eliminate or delegate the rest.

Another powerful strategy is time-blocking. By scheduling uninterrupted blocks of time for your most important tasks, you protect your focus and ensure that you are prioritizing the activities that truly matter. For example, block off time each day for strategic thinking, for deep work, or for creative endeavors. These time blocks become sacred, and you avoid allowing trivial tasks to crowd them out. When you simplify your schedule, you reclaim time and energy to focus on your most impactful work.

Decluttering Your Environment: Creating a Space That Supports Your Leadership

A cluttered environment can lead to a cluttered mind. When your physical space is disorganized or filled with distractions, it's hard to maintain clarity or focus. In order to lead effectively, you need a space that supports your mental clarity and allows you to work without constant interruptions.

Take the time to evaluate your workspace. Is it conducive to the work you need to do? Is it cluttered with papers, gadgets, or items that distract you? A clean, organized environment can make a world of difference in how you feel and perform. Simplify your surroundings by removing items that don't serve you. Organize your workspace so that you can easily find what you need and stay focused on the task at hand.

This doesn't just apply to your office; your home environment is just as important. Creating a peaceful, organized home space helps you feel grounded and recharged, which is essential for your well-being and your leadership. Simplifying your environment is an act of self-care, allowing you to restore energy so that you can be more present and focused when you're working.

Mental Subtraction: Letting Go of Unnecessary Thoughts and Beliefs

Simplification doesn't just apply to your physical space—it also applies to your mental and emotional landscape. Many of us carry around mental clutter in the form of negative thoughts, limiting beliefs, and unnecessary worries. These mental distractions drain our energy and prevent us from being fully present. They also cloud our decision-making, making it harder to lead with clarity and confidence.

One of the most powerful ways to simplify your mental space is through **mindfulness**. Practicing mindfulness allows you to observe your thoughts without attachment or judgment. When you catch yourself spiraling into worry or doubt, take a step back and ask yourself: "Is this thought serving me? Is it helping me make better decisions or leading me toward my goals?" If not, gently release it. This process of letting go of unnecessary thoughts frees up mental space for focus, creativity, and strategic thinking.

Another way to simplify your mind is by examining your beliefs. How many of your beliefs are helping you grow, and how many are holding you back? Do you have limiting beliefs about your potential, your worth, or your ability to lead? Subtracting these limiting beliefs allows you to step into your full power as a leader. Shift your mindset from one of scarcity or fear to one of abundance and possibility. The more you let go of old, unhelpful beliefs, the more room you create for new, empowering ones.

Emotional Subtraction: Letting Go of Toxicity

Another area of subtraction that can have a profound impact on your leadership is emotional subtraction. We all carry emotional baggage—negative feelings, grudges, past hurts—that can weigh us down and cloud our judgment. These emotional burdens can drain our energy and prevent us from leading with clarity and compassion.

Start by evaluating the relationships in your life. Are there people who drain your energy or cause unnecessary stress? Are there toxic dynamics that are affecting your emotional well-being? It's important to set boundaries in these relationships and, when necessary, let go of those who no longer serve your highest good. While it can be difficult, emotional subtraction is essential for your long-term well-being as a leader.

Similarly, let go of self-criticism or the pressure to be perfect. Striving for excellence is one thing, but perfectionism can lead to stress, burnout, and a lack of clarity. Practice self-compassion and allow yourself the grace to be human. When you stop holding yourself to unrealistic standards, you create emotional space for growth, creativity, and presence.

Subtraction as a Tool for Clarity and Focus

When we remove the unnecessary from our lives, we make room for what truly matters. Whether it's simplifying your schedule, decluttering your environment, letting go of limiting beliefs, or creating healthier emotional boundaries, subtraction is about creating space for clarity, focus, and purpose. It's about making sure that every action you take is aligned with your goals and your values.

By embracing the power of subtraction, you become more intentional with your time, energy, and focus. You can lead with greater presence, clarity, and confidence, knowing that everything you do is in service of your vision and your purpose.

Leadership is not about doing more; it's about doing what matters most with the energy and clarity that comes from living a simplified, intentional life. Embrace the power of subtraction, and you'll find that success comes not from adding more to your life but from stripping away what doesn't serve you. By simplifying your life, you create the space to lead with strength, resilience, and purpose.

******

Real-Life Examples of Effective Minimization in Personal and Professional Settings

Now that we've discussed the power of subtraction and how simplifying your life can enhance clarity and focus, it's time to look at some real-life examples of how effective minimization works in both personal and professional settings. The act of simplifying isn't just a theoretical concept—it's something that successful people across all walks of life practice consistently. By looking at how others have used subtraction to create more intentional, focused lives, you can see how these principles can be applied in your own journey as a leader.

1. Steve Jobs: Simplifying for Clarity and Impact

Steve Jobs, the co-founder of Apple, is often celebrated not only for his vision and creativity but also for his ability to simplify and focus on what truly matters. In both his personal life and professional endeavors, Jobs famously eliminated unnecessary distractions in order to stay focused on his biggest goals.

In terms of his professional life, Jobs took simplification to the extreme. He was known for his obsession with design and user experience, which led him to pare down the functions of Apple products to the essentials. He famously eliminated features that he felt distracted from the core experience. This focus on minimalism is reflected in the clean, simple design of Apple products, which are not only aesthetically pleasing but also intuitively functional.

Jobs also minimized distractions in his personal life. In his later years, he made conscious decisions to distance himself from certain relationships and commitments that no longer served his focus on building Apple into the global powerhouse it became. He was known for creating a space where he could focus his energy on what was most important to him. His ability to remove clutter—whether in his product designs, daily routine, or personal commitments—allowed him to maintain the clarity and focus needed to change the tech world.

The lesson here? Minimizing distractions and focusing on what's truly important in your leadership—whether it's the products you create, the people you lead, or the work you do—allows you to achieve far more than if you're constantly scattered in a hundred different directions.

2. Marie Kondo: Simplifying the Home to Create Mental Clarity

Marie Kondo, the organizing consultant and author of *The Life-Changing Magic of Tidying Up*, is a perfect example of how minimizing your environment can lead to a clearer, more focused mind. Her KonMari method, which encourages people to keep only the items that "spark joy," isn't just about decluttering your physical space. It's about creating an environment that supports your emotional and mental well-being.

Marie Kondo advocates for removing physical clutter in order to create a space that nurtures calm and clarity. Many of us are surrounded by things—clothes we never wear, papers we don't need, sentimental items that hold emotional weight, and random objects that pile up over time. Kondo's method encourages us to strip away these distractions and keep only the items that bring us peace or joy.

The effect of this decluttering is profound. By eliminating the excess in our environment, we free up both physical and mental space. In the workplace, a clean, organized environment can help you focus better and make clearer decisions. At home, it creates a sense of peace and restfulness, allowing you to recharge and approach your work with a clearer mind.

Kondo's work has become a global phenomenon because it taps into a basic human truth: simplifying our physical surroundings leads to greater mental and emotional clarity. By minimizing your space, you create room for the things and people that truly matter, both personally and professionally.

3. Warren Buffet: Saying No to Opportunities to Focus on What Matters

Warren Buffet, one of the wealthiest and most successful investors of all time, is known for his disciplined approach to work and life. Buffet's secret to success, according to him, lies in his ability to say no to nearly everything that isn't directly aligned with his core investment strategy. This is an excellent example of the power of minimizing distractions to focus on what truly drives success.

Buffet has famously said that the key to his success is saying no to "good opportunities" so he can focus on the "great ones." This philosophy allows him to direct his time and energy toward what he does best—investing in companies that he understands and that align with his long-term vision. By cutting out everything else, he has been able to focus on the few opportunities that truly align with his values and goals.

Buffet also takes a minimalist approach to his personal life. Despite his immense wealth, he lives in a modest home and leads a simple, straightforward lifestyle. He avoids distractions, focusing instead on his work and relationships that bring him joy and fulfillment. His ability to say no to distractions—whether in his professional or personal life—has allowed him to maintain the focus and clarity that has made him a business legend.

The lesson from Warren Buffet? In leadership, you can't do everything. Learning to say no to good opportunities so you can focus on great ones is key to staying clear, focused, and ultimately successful. By minimizing the number of commitments and distractions you allow into your life, you can better direct your energy toward the things that will make the most impact.

4. Shonda Rhimes: Saying No to Excess and Prioritizing Health and Family

Shonda Rhimes, the creator of hit TV shows like *Grey's Anatomy* and *Scandal*, had to learn the power of subtraction the hard way. In her book *Year of Yes*, Rhimes details how, for years, she said yes to everything—work, commitments, social obligations—at the expense of her health and her personal life. She found herself burned out, overwhelmed, and disconnected from her family.

In a moment of clarity, Rhimes realized she needed to make a change. She made the decision to say no to the things that didn't align with her priorities, which allowed her to focus on her health, her family, and her own happiness. By simplifying her schedule and prioritizing what mattered most, she was able to reclaim her energy, find joy in her work again, and rediscover balance in her life.

One powerful practice Rhimes adopted was carving out time for herself to rest and recharge, something that she had previously neglected. She made her health and well-being a priority, both for herself and for the sake of her family. In doing so, she became more present and focused in both her personal and professional life.

Rhimes' journey illustrates that sometimes the most powerful thing you can do as a leader is to subtract the unnecessary, whether it's work commitments, social obligations, or anything else that drains your energy. By simplifying your life and focusing on what truly matters, you set yourself up to lead with more joy, more balance, and greater impact.

5. The Minimalist Entrepreneur: Cutting Down on Tasks to Boost Productivity

In the world of entrepreneurship, the principle of subtraction is often a game-changer. Take the example of many successful minimalist entrepreneurs who intentionally simplify their business models and workflows to focus on what drives the most results. They cut out the tasks, services, or products that aren't yielding a good return on investment and double down on what works.

For example, one entrepreneur might choose to streamline their offerings, focusing on a single product or service that resonates most with their audience instead of spreading themselves thin with multiple product lines or services. Another may cut out time-consuming, low-value activities—like attending every networking event or answering every email—choosing instead to focus on high-leverage tasks that move the needle forward.

Minimalism in entrepreneurship isn't just about scaling back for the sake of scaling back; it's about creating the freedom to focus on what truly matters—whether that's building a strong customer base, improving product quality, or cultivating meaningful business relationships. By minimizing distractions and unnecessary tasks, these entrepreneurs create the time and mental space they need to innovate, grow, and lead effectively.

The Power of Subtraction: A Leadership Game-Changer

As we've seen from these real-life examples, subtraction isn't a passive act—it's a powerful leadership tool that can help you clear the clutter from your life and focus on what truly matters. Whether you're following Steve Jobs' approach to product design, Marie Kondo's method for decluttering your space, Warren Buffet's disciplined approach to saying no, or Shonda Rhimes' commitment to prioritizing health and family, the principle is the same: less is often more.

When you intentionally subtract distractions, excess commitments, and unnecessary stressors, you make room for clarity, creativity, and focus. And this, in turn, allows you to lead with greater impact, resilience, and purpose. The power of subtraction lies not just in what you remove but in the space you create for the things that truly matter.

So, as you move forward in your leadership journey, remember that simplifying your life isn't a sign of weakness—it's a powerful step toward leading with strength, clarity, and intention. Embrace the power of subtraction, and watch how your life—and leadership—become more focused, more purposeful, and more successful.

Chapter 7

Setting Healthy Boundaries

As female leaders, we are often juggling a multitude of responsibilities—leading teams, meeting deadlines, managing personal obligations, and trying to maintain a semblance of balance in our lives. It's easy to get caught up in the hustle and start saying "yes" to everything that comes our way. We often think that if we don't take on every task, every meeting, or every request, we might fall short or let someone down. But here's the truth: without clear boundaries, you're setting yourself up for burnout, frustration, and a lack of presence in your leadership.

Setting healthy boundaries—whether in your workload or your personal space—is not just about saying no to others; it's about saying yes to yourself. It's about creating a space in which you can show up fully, lead with clarity, and protect your energy. Boundaries allow you to focus on what matters most, be more present with your teams and loved ones, and maintain your well-being.

In this chapter, we'll explore why boundaries are essential for your leadership, how they support your personal and professional life, and how to set and maintain boundaries that empower you to lead with strength, resilience, and authenticity.

The Power of Boundaries in Leadership

As a leader, your ability to manage your energy, time, and resources directly impacts how effectively you lead. Without boundaries, your energy gets depleted by endless demands, and your time is consumed by tasks that drain you rather than move you toward your goals. Boundaries are the protective force that keeps your energy intact and allows you to direct your focus where it's most needed.

Boundaries are often misunderstood as rigid walls that shut people out. In reality, healthy boundaries are flexible and dynamic, allowing you to maintain control over your life while still being available and supportive to others. They are not about cutting people off or shutting down communication; they're about defining where your responsibilities end and where others begin. When you have clear boundaries, you can be fully present in both your work and your personal life—because you've made space for both.

Think of boundaries as the limits that preserve your capacity to lead. They allow you to prioritize the right tasks, focus on what truly moves the needle, and say no to things that drain your time and energy. Boundaries are a form of self-care that support your long-term health, productivity, and peace of mind. Without them, you risk losing your sense of direction, feeling overwhelmed, and ultimately, burning out.

Why Boundaries Are Vital for Managing Your Workload

One of the most significant areas where boundaries are essential is managing your workload. As a leader, you are constantly faced with competing priorities, urgent deadlines, and requests from colleagues or clients. Without clear boundaries, it's easy to get caught in the trap of trying to do everything, often sacrificing your own well-being in the process.

Without boundaries, you may find yourself working late into the night, sacrificing weekends, or saying yes to requests that don't align with your goals. Over time, this can lead to burnout, stress, and decreased effectiveness as a leader. But when you set boundaries around your workload, you reclaim control over your time and energy.

To establish boundaries around your work, start by assessing where you're spending your time and where it might be getting hijacked. Do you often find yourself working on tasks that aren't aligned with your key priorities? Are you saying yes to meetings or projects that don't move the needle forward for your team or business?

A simple but powerful boundary-setting strategy is the **"Say No to Say Yes"** approach. This means being intentional about what you say yes to by first saying no to anything that doesn't align with your vision or priorities. For example, instead of automatically accepting every meeting invitation, assess whether your attendance will add value or help you achieve your goals. If not, politely decline or delegate the responsibility to someone else.

You can also set boundaries around your work hours. If your workday tends to bleed into the evenings or weekends, set a firm end time for your workday. Communicate this boundary to your team, and stick to it. If you find yourself consistently working beyond those hours, assess why that's happening. Are you overcommitting? Are you taking on too many tasks that could be delegated? Setting and honoring work boundaries protects your time, preserves your energy, and helps you show up as your best self when it's time to work.

Personal Space: Protecting Your Energy and Well-Being

While managing your workload is crucial, personal space is just as important. As a leader, you need to protect not only your professional time but also your personal space. You cannot give to others if you are running on empty. Your personal life—whether it's time with family, relaxation, self-care, or hobbies—requires the same level of attention as your work.

Too often, leaders neglect their personal space, believing that they must always be available to their teams or clients. But this constant availability can erode your well-being. Just as you set boundaries around work tasks, you must also establish limits around your personal time. Without this separation, you risk burning out, feeling overwhelmed, and losing sight of what truly matters.

Personal boundaries might include setting limits on when and how you engage with work outside of office hours. For example, you could designate specific times when you are available to answer emails or take calls and establish clear times when you are not. This creates space for you to recharge, connect with loved ones, or simply enjoy some time to yourself.

Another important aspect of personal space is knowing when to disconnect. Technology has made it possible to be "on" at all times, but this constant connection can leave you feeling mentally drained. Set boundaries around your use of technology—whether that's limiting social media time or creating technology-free zones (like the dining table or your bedroom). Disconnecting from digital noise allows you to be more present with the people and activities that bring you joy and fulfillment.

When you protect your personal space, you not only protect your energy but also model healthy boundary-setting for those around you. As a leader, your well-being is essential to the success of your team. By taking time to recharge and protect your personal space, you are showing others that self-care and boundaries are necessary for sustainable success.

How to Set Healthy Boundaries in Relationships

Another area where boundaries are essential is in your relationships—whether with family, friends, or colleagues. Setting boundaries in relationships ensures that you maintain healthy, respectful interactions while also protecting your time and energy. It's important to communicate openly with others about your needs and limitations.

One way to set healthy boundaries in relationships is by being clear about your availability. For example, if a colleague frequently asks for your time outside of work hours, communicate your limits by letting them know when you are available to help and when you need personal time. The same goes for family and friends—if you need downtime, let them know in advance and set aside specific times for socializing or family activities. Clear communication helps avoid misunderstandings and ensures that everyone's needs are respected.

Setting boundaries doesn't mean being distant or unkind. It simply means being intentional about how much time and energy you give to others and making sure that it aligns with your priorities. When you establish healthy boundaries, you create space for meaningful, fulfilling relationships that nurture your well-being instead of draining you.

******

Strategies to Implement and Maintain Effective Boundaries

Now that we've discussed the importance of setting healthy boundaries for your workload, personal space, and relationships, let's dive into the actionable strategies you can use to implement and maintain those boundaries effectively. It's one thing to recognize the need for boundaries—it's another to actually put them into practice and keep them intact, especially when pressures arise or when others try to push past your limits.

The key to successful boundary-setting lies in clarity, consistency, and self-awareness. These strategies will help you define your boundaries, communicate them effectively, and protect them, ensuring that you maintain your well-being, focus, and energy as you continue to lead.

1. Clarify Your Priorities and Values

The first step in setting effective boundaries is to get crystal clear about your own priorities and values. When you know what truly matters to you, it becomes much easier to identify where you need to set limits and say no to things that don't align with your goals.

Start by reflecting on your leadership vision and personal values. What is most important to you in your work and in your life? What are the goals and outcomes that you want to focus on? For example, is your top priority being present with your family? Is it fostering a healthy, high-performing team? Or is it maintaining a work-life balance that allows you to thrive physically, mentally, and spiritually?

When you have a clear sense of your priorities, it's much easier to create boundaries that protect your time and energy. Boundaries are not just about saying no to others—they are about saying yes to the things that truly support your vision. When you're clear on your priorities, saying no becomes much easier, and saying yes to what matters most becomes more natural.

2. Be Clear and Direct in Communicating Your Boundaries

Once you've identified your boundaries, it's time to communicate them clearly and confidently to those around you—whether it's your team, colleagues, clients, or even family members. The key here is to be direct but also respectful and professional.

For example, if you've decided to limit your work hours and avoid checking emails after 6 p.m., communicate that expectation clearly to your team. Let them know that while you are fully committed during working hours, your evenings are reserved for personal time and family. Be upfront about your limits and set clear expectations for when you will or won't be available. The clearer you are, the less confusion or pushback you will face later.

It's important to communicate your boundaries consistently. This is particularly important when you're working with others who may be used to having unrestricted access to you. Don't be afraid to reinforce your boundaries if they are tested. Consistency is key in maintaining boundaries, and you'll quickly establish a culture of respect when you're clear about your needs.

3. Learn the Power of "No"

One of the most important tools in your boundary-setting toolkit is the power of the word "no." Saying no is often seen as a negative or unkind response, but in reality, it is one of the most powerful and positive things you can do for yourself. Saying no doesn't mean you're rejecting others; it means you're protecting your time, energy, and focus.

Learning how to say no gracefully is a skill every leader must master. When someone asks you to take on a new project, attend a meeting, or get involved in something outside of your primary responsibilities, ask yourself: Does this align with my priorities? Will it move me closer to my goals? If the answer is no, politely decline. You don't need to provide a long explanation—sometimes, a simple "I'm unable to take that on at this time" or "That doesn't fit within my current priorities" is enough.

Practice saying no in low-stakes situations first. For example, if a colleague asks for help on a project that's outside your focus, practice saying no in a respectful way: "I wish I could assist, but I'm focused on other priorities at the moment." Over time, you'll become more comfortable asserting your boundaries, and you'll start to see the benefits of maintaining them.

4. Create Rituals for Transitioning Between Roles

One of the biggest challenges in maintaining boundaries is the constant shifting between different roles—being a leader, a colleague, a spouse, a parent, or a friend. The mental and emotional energy required to switch between these roles can be exhausting, and without boundaries, it's easy to feel like you're never fully present in any one area.

One effective strategy is to create rituals that help you transition between roles. For example, at the end of your workday, take a few minutes to decompress before jumping into family or personal time. This could mean going for a walk, practicing deep breathing, or even spending a few minutes reflecting on your workday. Similarly, if you're moving from family time into work mode, have a ritual to mentally shift gears—such as reviewing your schedule for the day or setting an intention for your work.

These rituals create a mental boundary that helps you close the door on one role and open the door to another. They also allow you to be more present and focused when you're in each role without feeling like you're constantly juggling or spreading yourself too thin.

5. Delegate to Create Space

Another powerful way to maintain boundaries is to delegate. As a leader, you don't have to do everything yourself. One of the most effective ways to protect your time and energy is to trust your team and empower them to take on responsibilities that don't require your direct involvement.

Delegating tasks doesn't just lighten your load; it also helps your team members grow and develop. By giving others ownership of tasks, you create a more balanced workload for yourself while fostering a culture of trust and empowerment within your team. Delegation can be a difficult skill to learn, especially for perfectionists or leaders who feel like they need to be involved in every decision. But when you let go of the need to control everything, you free up time and space to focus on the areas that truly need your attention.

Start by identifying tasks that can be handled by others—whether it's routine administrative work, research, or even decision-making in certain areas. Empower others by giving them the tools, guidance, and confidence to take on these responsibilities. The more you delegate, the more you'll create the space you need to lead effectively without burning out.

6. Protect Your Time with Non-Negotiables

Another way to maintain your boundaries is to establish non-negotiable commitments in your schedule. These are the things that are sacred—your time for exercise, your time with family, your personal self-care, or your strategic thinking time. These are the areas where you can't afford to compromise because they're foundational to your health and leadership.

Once you've identified these non-negotiables, protect them fiercely. Don't allow work or other people's demands to override them. Schedule them into your calendar just as you would an important meeting or deadline, and treat them as a priority. This might mean saying no to certain work requests, avoiding back-to-back meetings, or ensuring you leave the office at a reasonable hour. Your time is precious, and when you create non-negotiable time blocks for your personal and professional well-being, you ensure that you're leading with your best energy and focus.

7. Use Technology to Your Advantage

In today's fast-paced world, technology can be a double-edged sword. It has the power to help you stay organized and productive, but it can also blur the lines between work and personal life, making it harder to maintain boundaries.

Use technology to create and maintain your boundaries. Set email filters and notifications to avoid getting caught in a constant cycle of checking emails. Use scheduling tools to block off time for deep work or personal activities, and set boundaries around your availability. For example, consider using the "Do Not Disturb" feature on your phone or computer during your off-hours or when you're engaged in focused work.

Technology can be a tool for maintaining boundaries, but it's essential to use it intentionally. By leveraging these tools, you can create a digital environment that supports your efforts to protect your time and energy.

8. Practice Self-Compassion and Flexibility

Finally, it's important to remember that setting boundaries isn't always perfect. There will be times when life happens, when emergencies arise, or when you need to be flexible. It's important to practice self-compassion during these moments and not beat yourself up if you need to adjust your boundaries.

Self-compassion allows you to recognize that you are doing the best you can and that it's okay to recalibrate. Flexibility doesn't mean abandoning your boundaries—it means being kind to yourself when things don't go as planned and giving yourself permission to adjust when necessary.

The Ongoing Practice of Boundary-Setting

Implementing and maintaining healthy boundaries is an ongoing process, not a one-time event. It requires self-awareness, discipline, and the ability to communicate your needs clearly. By setting and protecting your boundaries, you are ensuring that you have the energy, focus, and presence to lead with authenticity and strength.

As you continue on your leadership journey, remember that boundaries are not a sign of weakness or limitation—they are a powerful tool for creating space, protecting your well-being, and ensuring that you show up as the best version of yourself for your team, your family, and yourself. Keep refining your boundaries, stay true to your priorities, and watch how your leadership—and your life—become more intentional, impactful, and fulfilling.

Chapter 8

The Power in Having a Routine

In the hustle and bustle of leadership, we often feel like we're constantly putting out fires, responding to urgent emails, and reacting to everything that comes our way. The demands can be overwhelming, and we may find ourselves working harder but not necessarily smarter. In moments like these, it's easy to think that productivity comes from sheer willpower and the ability to juggle a million things at once. But here's the truth: the most effective leaders don't rely on chaos—they rely on structure.

The power of having a routine cannot be overstated. A routine isn't just a set of habits; it's a strategic tool that empowers you to stay focused, reduce stress, and maximize your productivity. By creating a routine, you eliminate the mental strain of constantly deciding what to do next, and you ensure that your day is aligned with your priorities. Routines streamline your life, help you stay grounded, and allow you to perform at your best, day in and day out.

In this chapter, we'll explore how routines contribute to efficiency, reduce stress, and foster a sense of control. We'll also look at how you can create a routine that supports your goals, boosts your energy, and enhances your leadership potential.

The Science Behind Routines: Why They Work

At their core, routines are about creating structure. But why does structure have such a profound impact on our productivity and well-being?

The answer lies in the way our brains work. Every time we make a decision—whether it's what to eat for lunch, what task to tackle next, or whether to check our phone—we expend mental energy. This constant decision-making leads to decision fatigue, a phenomenon where our ability to make sound choices diminishes as the day goes on. Decision fatigue can result in procrastination, poor judgment, and overwhelm. When we have to make too many decisions, we end up wasting valuable energy, which can affect our overall efficiency.

This is where routines come in. By establishing a set routine, we remove the need to make decisions about what comes next. We've already decided ahead of time. Our brains don't need to work overtime on trivial decisions, freeing up mental energy for more important tasks. This structure enables us to flow through our day with greater ease, knowing exactly what to do and when to do it.

Studies have shown that routines help reduce stress by providing predictability. When our days are structured and our expectations are clear, we feel more in control and less anxious about what's coming next. Routines give us a sense of purpose and direction, reducing the mental load and allowing us to focus on what really matters.

How Routines Contribute to Efficiency

A well-designed routine can make a world of difference in how efficient you are as a leader. The key to efficiency lies in consistency. When you have a set routine, you don't waste time trying to figure out what to do next or how to organize your day. Your mind and body know exactly what to expect, and you can dive straight into the work that matters most.

One of the main benefits of a routine is that it helps you prioritize your time. A solid routine forces you to plan ahead, ensuring that your most important tasks come first. You don't just let your day unfold haphazardly—you proactively decide what needs to be done and when. For example, setting aside a block of time in the morning for strategic thinking or deep work allows you to accomplish your most critical tasks before distractions set in.

Routines also help you break down larger goals into manageable steps. Instead of feeling overwhelmed by the magnitude of a project or responsibility, you can break it down into smaller tasks and schedule them throughout your day or week. This makes the entire process more manageable and keeps you on track rather than leaving you scrambling at the last minute.

In addition, having a routine eliminates the need for constant reorganization. When you don't have a routine, you might find yourself jumping between tasks, trying to catch up, or playing catch-up with emails and meetings. A routine provides a framework that reduces the mental clutter and minimizes the time spent on figuring out what comes next.

Routines Reduce Stress by Creating Predictability

One of the most powerful benefits of having a routine is its ability to reduce stress. As leaders, we often face unexpected challenges, tight deadlines, and the weight of important decisions. However, when the day-to-day elements of our lives are predictable and structured, it creates a sense of stability and control. This predictability is a crucial antidote to stress.

Think about the simple act of having a morning routine. When you wake up and know exactly how you'll start your day—whether it's with a morning stretch, a healthy breakfast, a quiet moment of reflection, or a walk outside—you're setting yourself up for success. This small act of consistency in your morning routine helps set the tone for the rest of the day. It establishes a sense of calm and order before the whirlwind of responsibilities and distractions begins.

On the flip side, when you don't have a routine, your day can feel chaotic. You might find yourself rushing from task to task, feeling overwhelmed by the lack of structure. Routines bring a sense of calm, helping you stay focused even when life around you feels uncertain or stressful.

By establishing a routine, you also build in self-care and downtime. For example, setting aside time for exercise, meditation, or reading each day not only supports your physical and mental health but also allows you to recharge and refocus. When these activities are built into your routine, you're less likely to let them fall by the wayside due to busyness or stress. They become non-negotiable parts of your day that ensure you're operating at your highest potential.

Routines Promote Healthy Habits

When you establish a routine, you're also creating the conditions for building positive habits. Consistency is key to habit formation, and routines provide the structure that helps you reinforce good habits over time. Whether it's exercising regularly, eating nutritious meals, prioritizing sleep, or carving out time for self-reflection, routines support these habits by making them an integral part of your daily life.

Take exercise, for example. When you make physical activity a non-negotiable part of your daily routine, it becomes something you do automatically—just like brushing your teeth. You don't have to think about whether you'll exercise today or make excuses. It's already built into your routine, and you've prioritized it as part of your health and leadership strategy.

The same goes for other habits that support your well-being and leadership. Whether it's setting aside time to read, journaling, or having a daily moment of gratitude, these small practices accumulate over time, contributing to your overall growth and success. Routines help you create a foundation for these habits to thrive, which ultimately leads to greater well-being, productivity, and focus.

Building a Routine That Supports Your Leadership Goals

Now that we've covered the benefits of having a routine, let's look at how you can build one that supports your leadership goals. The key to creating an effective routine is ensuring that it aligns with your values, priorities, and energy levels.

1. **Identify Your Priorities**: What matters most to you as a leader? What are the key activities that will help you achieve your personal and professional goals? Make sure your routine is designed around these priorities. For example, if strategic thinking is crucial for your leadership, block out uninterrupted time each day for deep work or creative thinking.

2. **Start Small**: It's tempting to want to overhaul your entire day and introduce a new routine all at once, but this can be overwhelming. Start by incorporating small, manageable habits into your routine. Over time, you can build and expand on these habits until they become second nature.

3. **Make It Sustainable**: A successful routine is one you can maintain in the long term. Be realistic about your commitments and energy levels. Don't try to fit in too many tasks in one day. Instead, focus on consistency and creating a routine that you can stick to, even on busy or stressful days.

4. **Create Morning and Evening Rituals**: Your morning and evening routines set the tone for the day. Start your day with a ritual that prepares you mentally, emotionally, and physically for the challenges ahead. Similarly, end your day with a ritual that helps you unwind, reflect, and recharge.

5. **Be Flexible**: Life is unpredictable, and there will be times when your routine needs to adjust. It's important to remain flexible and not beat yourself up if things don't go as planned. The goal is not perfection; the goal is consistency. Allow yourself the flexibility to adapt when necessary, but always return to the core habits that support your leadership.

Conclusion: Leading with the Power of Routine

Having a routine is not about restricting your freedom or adding another layer of structure to your life. It's about creating a framework that supports your highest potential as a leader. A routine helps you conserve mental energy, reduce stress, and stay focused on what truly matters. It builds healthy habits that reinforce your well-being and ensure you're always operating at your best.

As you continue on your leadership journey, remember that routines are your ally. They provide clarity, consistency, and a sense of control in a world that often feels chaotic and unpredictable. When you commit to a routine that aligns with your values and priorities, you set yourself up for greater efficiency, reduced stress, and long-term success.

******

Developing and Sticking to Routines That Bolster Productivity

Creating a routine is one thing—but sticking to it is where the real power lies. In the fast-paced, high-pressure world of leadership, it's easy for your best intentions to fall by the wayside when urgent tasks and unexpected demands take over. However, by developing routines that bolster productivity and making them a non-negotiable part of your day, you can overcome the temptation to be reactive and instead become proactive, focused, and intentional in your work.

A productivity-boosting routine is not just a list of tasks to check off. It's a carefully designed structure that allows you to work smarter, not harder, and ensures that your time and energy are channeled into the activities that will drive your leadership success. In this section, we'll dive into how to create routines that help you maximize your productivity, stay focused on your priorities, and build habits that support your long-term goals. We'll also explore how to stay committed to those routines, even when life gets busy or challenging.

1. Start with Your "Big Rocks"—Prioritize What Matters Most

The first step in developing a productive routine is identifying your top priorities—the big rocks. In leadership, these are the tasks or activities that will move you closest to your goals and that align with your core values. Without a clear sense of what matters most, it's easy to get caught up in the whirlwind of everyday demands, leaving little time for strategic thinking, creative work, or personal development.

To ensure your routine is productivity-focused, begin each day or week by identifying the "big rocks"—the key tasks or projects that deserve your time and attention. These might include things like:

- Strategic planning for your team or business

- Deep work on a critical project or goal

- Meetings with key stakeholders

- Personal development activities, such as reading, learning, or reflecting

Once you've identified these key priorities, schedule them into your routine first, before any less critical tasks or meetings. By placing these "big rocks" at the start of your day or week, you make sure they get the attention they deserve. This ensures that your routine is aligned with what matters most, rather than getting bogged down in small, less important tasks.

2. Time-Blocking: Protecting Your Most Productive Hours

Time-blocking is one of the most effective strategies for building a productivity-enhancing routine. Time-blocking involves scheduling specific chunks of time for different tasks, activities, or projects throughout your day. This method eliminates the mental clutter of trying to figure out what to do next, and it helps you dedicate focused time to your most important priorities.

To implement time-blocking, start by identifying your peak productivity hours. For most people, these are the early hours of the day, but it varies depending on your energy levels and work style. Once you know when you're most focused, block off that time for your most critical tasks—like strategic thinking, creative work, or problem-solving. Treat these blocks as sacred, and avoid scheduling meetings or answering emails during these periods.

Throughout the rest of your day, block off time for other key activities, like checking email, holding meetings, or attending to administrative tasks. Be sure to include time for breaks and personal activities as well—these moments of rest are essential for maintaining focus and preventing burnout.

Time-blocking allows you to create a sense of structure, ensuring that you stay on track with your goals and don't get sidetracked by distractions or less important tasks. It also helps you avoid the trap of multitasking, which can reduce efficiency and mental clarity.

3. Build in Breaks and Downtime: The Power of Rest

One of the most common misconceptions about productivity is that the more you work, the more you accomplish. But the truth is that working non-stop without taking breaks is a recipe for burnout, fatigue, and reduced focus. In fact, taking regular breaks is essential for maintaining high productivity over the long term.

When creating your routine, be sure to build in time for breaks. This can be as simple as a 5-minute walk after a focused work block or a 30-minute lunch break to recharge. Research has shown that taking breaks throughout the day improves cognitive function, creativity, and focus. The Pomodoro Technique, which involves working in 25-minute intervals followed by a 5-minute break, is one popular method that promotes productivity while allowing for regular rest.

Downtime isn't just about resting your body; it's about giving your brain the space to process and recharge. For instance, after a period of intense focus, a brief walk in nature or a meditation session can help clear mental clutter and restore clarity. Regular breaks allow you to return to your work with a fresh perspective, renewed energy, and a sharper focus.

By incorporating breaks into your routine, you ensure that you can sustain your productivity over a longer period without risking burnout. Remember, rest is just as important as work, and scheduling intentional downtime into your day will ultimately make you more effective and focused when you're working.

4. Use Rituals and Routines to Reinforce Productivity

Rituals and routines are the backbone of a productivity-enhancing routine. These are the consistent habits and behaviors that signal to your brain it's time to focus, take action, or relax. By embedding rituals into your day, you remove the need to make decisions about what comes next, allowing you to stay focused on your work rather than being distracted by the question, "What should I do now?"

Start by creating a morning routine that sets you up for a productive day. This could include activities such as:

- A short meditation or breathing exercise to center yourself

- A brief workout or stretch to get your body moving

- A healthy breakfast to fuel your body

- A review of your top priorities for the day

These morning rituals signal to your brain that it's time to focus, helping you transition smoothly into your workday. Similarly, creating an evening routine helps you wind down and reflect on the day. This might involve reviewing what you accomplished, setting intentions for the next day, and ensuring you're taking time for rest and self-care.

Having rituals in place ensures that your day flows smoothly, minimizing decision fatigue and allowing you to stay on track with your productivity goals.

5. Set Realistic Expectations and Avoid Perfectionism

One of the biggest obstacles to maintaining a productive routine is perfectionism. It's easy to fall into the trap of thinking that your routine has to be flawless or that you have to accomplish everything on your to-do list. But the truth is perfectionism often leads to procrastination and stress.

When developing a routine, aim for progress, not perfection. Start by setting realistic expectations about what you can accomplish in a day. Break your tasks into manageable steps, and focus on completing them one at a time rather than overwhelming yourself with an unrealistic list of goals.

It's also important to recognize that life will sometimes throw curveballs. You may not always be able to follow your routine exactly as planned, and that's okay. Be flexible and kind to yourself when things don't go as expected. The key is consistency, not perfection. If you miss a block of time or a task doesn't get completed, simply adjust and move forward without judgment.

6. Evaluate and Adjust Your Routine Regularly

Your routine is not set in stone. Over time, your priorities, goals, and energy levels may change, and your routine should reflect that. Regularly evaluate how your routine is serving you and whether it's helping you achieve the outcomes you want. Are you feeling more focused? Are you getting the right work done? Are you managing your energy effectively?

Take time every few weeks or months to reflect on your routine and make adjustments as needed. Perhaps you need to change the times when you do deep work, add more time for personal activities, or shift your focus to new priorities. The goal is to keep your routine fluid and adaptable so that it continues to support your productivity and well-being.

Conclusion: The Power of Consistency and Focus

Developing and sticking to routines that bolster productivity is a powerful tool for any leader. By implementing time-blocking, creating productive rituals, setting realistic expectations, and building in breaks and rest, you ensure that your time and energy are focused on what truly matters. Routines provide structure, reduce stress, and allow you to perform at your highest level.

The most successful leaders know that productivity isn't about doing more; it's about doing what matters most with clarity and intention. A solid routine creates the space to focus on your big goals while keeping distractions and stress at bay. When you commit to a routine that aligns with your priorities and supports your personal and professional growth, you empower yourself to lead with focus, efficiency, and purpose.

Chapter 9

Have Some Play Time

As leaders, we are often driven by ambition, purpose, and the relentless pursuit of our goals. We set high standards for ourselves, push through obstacles, and give our best in everything we do. But here's the reality: even the most driven and successful leaders need downtime. Time to rest, recharge, and simply *play*.

In a culture that often glorifies constant hustle and productivity, taking time for play can feel counterintuitive. It may even seem like a waste of time, especially when there are so many tasks waiting for your attention. But in truth, play is not only essential for your personal well-being, it's also a critical part of your leadership strategy. Downtime is where your creativity, innovation, and resilience are nurtured. It's during these moments of rest and relaxation that your brain processes information, generates new ideas, and allows you to step back and gain perspective. Without play, we risk burnout, diminished creativity, and the loss of passion for what we do.

In this chapter, we'll explore the critical role of downtime in fostering creative thinking, sustaining long-term productivity, and ensuring the longevity of your leadership. We'll also dive into how you can intentionally create space for play in your life and why doing so will make you a better, more effective leader.

The Power of Downtime for Creative Thinking

It might seem like the busier you are, the more creative you need to be. After all, as a leader, you're constantly solving problems, making decisions, and thinking strategically. However, research has shown that the best ideas often come when we step away from the pressure of constant work. In fact, creativity thrives in moments of rest and relaxation.

When we take breaks, our brains enter what's called the **default mode network**—a state of mind that allows our minds to wander and make new connections. It's in this relaxed state that our most creative ideas often emerge. For instance, you may find that your best ideas come to you during a walk, a shower, or while driving—moments when your mind is free to roam and connect dots without the weight of immediate deadlines or tasks. Downtime allows you to step away from the noise and let your mind engage in creative problem-solving without the constraints of structured thinking.

One of the greatest myths about creativity is that it requires constant work and discipline. But the reality is that creativity flourishes in an environment of relaxation and play. The more we allow ourselves time to rest, the more our minds have the space to form new ideas, challenge assumptions, and approach problems from fresh perspectives.

As a leader, giving yourself permission to play isn't just an indulgence—it's an investment in your creativity and innovative thinking. By intentionally carving out time for activities that recharge you, you can return to your work with renewed energy, sharper ideas, and a greater capacity to lead with vision and insight.

Play and the Longevity of Leadership

Leadership, especially over the long term, requires stamina. It's not just about burning bright for a short period; it's about sustaining your energy, creativity, and drive over the years. This is where play and downtime are crucial. Without rest, you risk burnout—an emotional, physical, and mental depletion that can diminish your ability to lead effectively.

Studies have shown that prolonged stress without adequate recovery leads to a significant decrease in both physical and mental performance. If we don't give ourselves permission to rest, the body and mind will eventually shut down or force us to slow down in ways we don't expect. The result? We end up less productive, less creative, and less effective in our leadership.

Play, on the other hand, rejuvenates us. It's not about being idle; it's about engaging in activities that refresh our minds and bodies so we can show up with energy and enthusiasm. Downtime provides the recovery that allows us to work harder and smarter when we are engaged in our tasks. It's during these moments of rest that we restore our capacity to lead with resilience, patience, and clarity.

Think about the long game of leadership. Sustaining a high level of performance and engagement over decades requires periods of recovery. The most successful leaders understand this and intentionally make space for play and relaxation. They know that their creative energy, problem-solving skills, and leadership effectiveness depend on their ability to rest and recharge. By prioritizing downtime, you protect the longevity of your leadership and ensure that you have the energy and passion to keep moving forward.

The Emotional Benefits of Downtime

Beyond the cognitive and physical benefits, downtime is essential for emotional well-being. Leadership can be emotionally taxing, especially when navigating challenges, conflicts, and high-stakes decisions. The emotional weight of leading a team, company, or organization can sometimes feel overwhelming. When you're constantly "on" and immersed in your responsibilities, it's easy to burn out emotionally.

Taking time for yourself—whether that's through hobbies, travel, spending time with loved ones, or simply doing nothing for a while—helps restore emotional balance. Play gives you the emotional space to step back from the intensity of leadership and reconnect with the things that bring you joy and peace. Whether it's a weekend getaway, an afternoon of hiking, or just curling up with a good book, moments of downtime allow you to disconnect from the pressures of leadership and recharge emotionally.

In fact, play has been shown to reduce stress hormones, lower anxiety, and improve mood. When you engage in activities that make you happy and relaxed, you're replenishing your emotional reserves. This emotional recharge is critical for maintaining a positive outlook and staying engaged with your work, your team, and your vision. Leaders who prioritize their emotional health are more resilient, compassionate, and effective in their roles.

The Role of Play in Building Team Culture

As a leader, it's not just about taking time for yourself—it's also about fostering an environment where play and downtime are valued by your team. Encouraging your team to take breaks, have fun, and engage in creative activities is essential for building a high-performing, innovative team culture. When leaders prioritize play, it signals to their teams that rest and relaxation are important for overall well-being and success.

In fact, many successful companies and teams incorporate play into their organizational culture. Whether through team-building exercises, off-site retreats, or even casual social activities, these moments of fun and relaxation build camaraderie, trust, and creativity within teams. Play breaks down barriers, fosters collaboration, and sparks new ideas. By allowing your team to play, you give them the space to connect, recharge, and return to their work with renewed energy and focus.

As a leader, setting the tone for a playful, relaxed atmosphere can be one of the most powerful ways to enhance your team's productivity and creativity. Play doesn't diminish professionalism—it enhances it. When leaders and teams have the freedom to relax, laugh, and enjoy themselves, they bring more energy, passion, and innovation to their work.

How to Integrate Play into Your Routine

Incorporating play into your life doesn't have to be complicated or time-consuming. Play can be as simple as taking a walk outside, trying a new hobby, or spending quality time with friends or family. The key is to be intentional about scheduling time for activities that bring you joy and allow your mind to relax.

Here are a few simple ways to integrate play into your routine:

1. **Schedule Play Time**: Just like you schedule work meetings or strategic planning sessions, schedule play time in your calendar. Treat it as a non-negotiable part of your day or week.

2. **Engage in Physical Play**: Physical activities like hiking, dancing, or playing sports are great ways to relax and have fun while also recharging your body.

3. **Try Something New**: Whether it's a creative hobby, learning a new skill, or exploring a new place, trying something out of your usual routine stimulates your mind and provides a refreshing break from the usual tasks.

4. **Social Play**: Spend time with friends or family, engage in light-hearted conversations, or participate in activities that promote connection and laughter. These social interactions are a great way to lift your spirits and relieve stress.

5. **Unstructured Time**: Sometimes, the best play is unstructured time—the time when you don't have to "do" anything. Give yourself permission to do nothing and just enjoy the moment. Let your mind wander, be present, and see where it takes you.

Conclusion: Play is an Investment in Your Leadership

In leadership, it's easy to fall into the trap of believing that productivity equals success. But true leadership is about balance. Play, rest, and downtime are not luxuries—they are essential components of sustained success. When you give yourself permission to play, you create the mental, emotional, and physical space needed to be a more creative, resilient, and impactful leader.

Remember, creativity doesn't come from endless hours of work—it comes from moments of relaxation, joy, and connection. By incorporating play into your routine, you're investing in your well-being and your leadership longevity. Downtime allows you to recharge, think more clearly, and return to your leadership with renewed purpose and energy. So, take time to play. You'll be amazed at how it enhances your creativity, your effectiveness, and your ability to lead with passion and joy.

******

Balancing Hard Work with Meaningful Leisure Activities

As leaders, we often pride ourselves on our work ethic. We thrive on challenges, meet deadlines, and give our best effort in everything we do. But somewhere along the way, in the pursuit of success and progress, we often forget one critical thing: meaningful leisure activities are just as important as hard work. If we want to be at our best as leaders, we must learn how to balance the drive to succeed with the need for relaxation, recreation, and rejuvenation.

Leisure doesn't mean laziness. In fact, when approached intentionally, leisure activities can be incredibly restorative, enhancing creativity, reducing stress, and improving our overall well-being. But to experience these benefits, it's essential to choose leisure activities that bring genuine joy, fulfillment, and relaxation—activities that allow you to step away from your work without feeling guilty or disconnected.

In this chapter, we'll explore how balancing hard work with meaningful leisure activities can make you a more effective leader. You'll learn how to consciously integrate rest into your routine, the importance of setting aside time for yourself, and how to use leisure as a tool for boosting creativity, emotional resilience, and long-term productivity.

The Importance of Balancing Hard Work and Leisure

We live in a society that often values hard work above all else. The "hustle culture" encourages us to work longer hours, take on more responsibilities, and push ourselves to the limit. While hard work is essential to success, it's important to recognize that true productivity doesn't come from working non-stop. In fact, without proper balance, the constant grind can lead to burnout, reduced focus, and diminished creativity.

Leisure, on the other hand, provides the opportunity to recharge both mentally and physically. It allows us to step away from the stress and pressure of our responsibilities, giving our brains and bodies the space they need to restore themselves.

Research has shown that regular downtime and leisure activities are essential for maintaining optimal performance. They lower stress levels, increase cognitive function, and enhance emotional resilience. But it's not just about taking breaks—it's about intentionally integrating meaningful leisure into our lives. When we do this, we not only protect our energy but also create the conditions for creativity, fresh thinking, and renewed motivation.

As a leader, you need to model balance for those around you. By embracing leisure and rest, you're showing your team that taking time to recharge is not only okay but necessary for long-term success. Just as you prioritize your work, you must prioritize rest and recovery to ensure your continued effectiveness and longevity in your role.

Understanding Meaningful Leisure

The key to integrating leisure into your life isn't simply about "taking time off." It's about engaging in activities that provide genuine relaxation and fulfillment—activities that refresh you, spark joy, and help you disconnect from the pressures of leadership. It's about quality, not quantity.

Meaningful leisure activities are those that allow you to rest deeply while also giving you something valuable in return. This could be physical activities, creative pursuits, or even social experiences. The goal is to engage in activities that nourish your mind, body, and soul. Here are some examples of meaningful leisure:

- **Physical Activities**: Exercise isn't just for building strength—it's also a great way to clear your mind, boost your mood, and reduce stress. Whether it's hiking, yoga, swimming, or even just taking a walk in nature, moving your body helps restore energy and provides much-needed mental clarity.

- **Creative Hobbies**: Engaging in creative activities, like painting, writing, gardening, or cooking, allows you to express yourself and take a break from the analytical demands of leadership. These hobbies offer a sense of accomplishment and satisfaction that comes from doing something simply for the joy of it.

- **Spending Time with Loved Ones**: Meaningful leisure is also about connection. Whether it's a quiet dinner with family, a weekend getaway with friends, or a phone call with someone you care about, socializing and nurturing relationships provide emotional support and happiness, which are critical for long-term well-being.

- **Mindfulness Practices**: Activities like meditation, journaling, or simply sitting in silence can help clear your mind and restore focus. These practices foster a sense of peace and perspective, which enhances your ability to handle stress and make thoughtful decisions.

The idea behind meaningful leisure is to engage in activities that genuinely recharge you—not just activities that feel like a temporary escape. Meaningful leisure doesn't just help you feel better in the moment; it sustains you in the long run, boosting your overall productivity, creativity, and resilience.

Creating Space for Leisure in Your Routine

The first step in balancing hard work with leisure is recognizing that both are necessary for your well-being and success. Once you understand this, you can begin to make space for leisure in your routine, just as you do for meetings, deadlines, and work tasks.

Start by scheduling leisure activities into your calendar. Just as you would block time for meetings or important tasks, prioritize your downtime. This doesn't mean it's not spontaneous—it means that you're intentionally creating space for relaxation, fun, and connection in your life.

Here are a few ways to build leisure into your routine:

1. **Plan Downtime in Advance**: Set aside regular breaks throughout the week for leisure activities. Whether it's a long weekend, a mid-week evening off, or an afternoon for a hobby you enjoy, make time for activities that allow you to recharge.

2. **Take "Mental Health" Breaks**: In addition to scheduled leisurse time, take small breaks throughout your workday. A five-minute walk, a short meditation session, or a quick conversation with a colleague can be enough to reset your mind and provide a burst of energy.

3. **Set Boundaries Around Work Hours**: Protect your personal time by setting clear boundaries around your work hours. Once your workday is over, disconnect from emails and work-related tasks. Allow yourself to unwind without feeling guilty about not working every minute.

4. **Incorporate Play into Team Culture**: As a leader, you can set the tone for your team by encouraging them to take breaks, enjoy leisure activities, and engage in play. This not only supports your team's well-being but also builds camaraderie and creativity within your group. A team that values work-life balance and downtime is likely to be more engaged, productive, and innovative.

Play and Creativity: A Symbiotic Relationship

Leisure and creativity are deeply connected. The brain works best when it has moments of rest and relaxation, allowing it to make new connections and solve problems in innovative ways. Play, whether it's physical, creative, or social, is crucial for maintaining mental and emotional agility.

When we step away from our work and allow ourselves time for leisure, our brains can process information more effectively. Often, the best ideas come when we're not actively working—during a walk, while cooking dinner, or even while relaxing in the bath. By engaging in leisure, we give ourselves the mental space to think creatively and approach problems from new angles.

This is why creativity thrives when we balance work with downtime. Play isn't just an indulgence—it's a necessary part of maintaining your creative flow and problem-solving abilities. As a leader, you need to protect your ability to think innovatively, and the best way to do that is to regularly engage in activities that nurture your creativity and provide rest for your mind.

The Long-Term Benefits of Leisure

The benefits of balancing hard work with leisure go beyond just short-term rest or relaxation. In the long term, taking regular breaks and prioritizing downtime contributes to the longevity of your leadership and career. When you build meaningful leisure into your life, you enhance your capacity to:

- **Sustain energy**: By resting and playing regularly, you restore your physical and mental energy, ensuring that you don't burn out and can continue to lead with vitality and enthusiasm.

- **Improve decision-making**: Downtime helps clear your mind, reduce stress, and restore mental clarity—key elements for making thoughtful, well-considered decisions.

- **Foster better relationships**: By making time for family, friends, and social activities, you create deeper, more meaningful connections, which provide emotional support and fulfillment.

- **Increase resilience**: Leisure time helps you manage stress more effectively and bounce back from setbacks with greater emotional strength and perspective.

Embrace the Balance of Hard Work and Play

In leadership, balance is everything. The most successful leaders don't operate in a constant state of hustle—they know when to push hard and when to pull back. Play and downtime are not just luxuries; they are essential to maintaining the energy, creativity, and resilience required for sustained leadership.

By consciously balancing hard work with meaningful leisure, you create a sustainable rhythm for your life and leadership. When you make time for rest, relaxation, and play, you return to your work with renewed focus, clarity, and energy. You lead more effectively, think more creatively, and inspire those around you to do the same.

So, remember: work hard, but play just as hard. Embrace the power of downtime, and watch how it transforms your leadership journey.

Chapter 10

Let's Sum It Up

As we reach the conclusion of part two of the book, it's important to pause and reflect on the key lessons we've explored about mastering life. Leadership is not just about how you show up at work—it's about how you show up in every area of your life. To lead effectively, you must first build a life framework that supports your well-being, growth, and long-term success. The strategies in this section weren't about achieving perfection or trying to do it all; they were about creating balance, clarity, and purpose in your daily life.

Mastering life is an ongoing process. It's about aligning your priorities, managing your energy, and embracing habits that help you thrive, not just survive. As we sum it all up, let's revisit the key takeaways from this journey toward building a life that supports sustained leadership success.

1. Simplify to Focus on What Matters Most

One of the most powerful lessons in mastering life is learning to simplify. As leaders, we're often pulled in many directions, but true success comes from focusing on what truly matters. In Chapter 6, we explored the *Power of Subtraction*—the idea that doing less can lead to achieving more. By removing unnecessary distractions, commitments, and clutter, you create the space needed to focus on your priorities.

Simplifying isn't about doing less for the sake of doing less—it's about being intentional. It's about saying no to the things that don't align with your vision so that you can say yes to what truly serves your goals and well-being. Whether it's streamlining your schedule, decluttering your environment, or letting go of limiting beliefs, simplifying your life allows you to lead with clarity and purpose.

Takeaway: Simplify your life by focusing on your highest priorities. Remove distractions and let go of what doesn't serve your goals so you can channel your energy into what truly matters.

2. Set and Protect Healthy Boundaries

Leadership requires energy, and without boundaries, it's easy to deplete yourself by saying yes to everything and everyone. In Chapter 7, we discussed the importance of *Setting Healthy Boundaries*. Boundaries are not barriers—they are tools that protect your time, energy, and mental space, allowing you to show up fully in your work and personal life.

Setting boundaries means being clear about your limits and communicating them effectively. It means learning to say no without guilt and prioritizing your well-being. When you establish boundaries around your workload, personal space, and relationships, you create a sustainable framework for success. Healthy boundaries are essential for maintaining focus, avoiding burnout, and staying aligned with your values.

Takeaway: Boundaries protect your ability to lead. By setting and maintaining clear limits, you preserve your energy, focus on your priorities, and show up as your best self.

3. Harness the Power of Routine

Routines are the foundation of a well-lived life. In Chapter 8, *The Power in Having a Routine*, we explored how routines contribute to efficiency, reduce stress, and create a sense of stability. When you establish a routine, you eliminate the need to constantly decide what to do next, freeing up mental energy for more important tasks.

A strong routine helps you prioritize your time, build positive habits, and maintain consistency in your leadership and personal life. It's not about creating rigid rules—it's about designing a framework that supports your goals and aligns with your values. Whether it's a morning ritual that sets the tone for the day or an evening routine that helps you unwind, routines allow you to lead with intention and focus.

Takeaway: Build routines that reflect your priorities and values. Consistency in your daily habits creates the stability and clarity needed to lead effectively.

4. Prioritize Rest and Play

Leadership is a marathon, not a sprint. To sustain your energy and creativity over the long term, you must prioritize rest and play. In Chapter 9, *Have Some Play Time*, we talked about the critical role of downtime in fostering creativity, resilience, and longevity. Play is not a luxury—it's an essential part of a balanced, fulfilling life.

Balancing hard work with meaningful leisure activities allows you to recharge, reduce stress, and return to your work with fresh energy and perspective. Whether it's engaging in a hobby, spending time in nature, or simply taking a break from technology, play nurtures your mind, body, and soul. It's during moments of rest and relaxation that your best ideas often emerge.

Takeaway: Rest and play are not indulgences—they are investments in your well-being and leadership. Make time for leisure and downtime to sustain your energy, creativity, and passion.

5. Align Your Life with Your Values

At the heart of mastering life is alignment. Everything you do—your routines, boundaries, goals, and downtime—should reflect your core values and priorities. Leadership is most powerful when it comes from a place of authenticity and purpose. By aligning your life with what truly matters to you, you create a sense of balance and fulfillment that sustains you in your leadership journey.

Alignment isn't about achieving perfection. It's about making conscious choices that support your vision and bring meaning to your work and personal life. When your actions are aligned with your values, you lead with integrity, inspire others, and stay grounded, even in the face of challenges.

Takeaway: Mastering life means aligning your daily actions with your core values. Let your priorities guide your decisions, and lead with authenticity and purpose.

Moving Forward: Embrace the Journey

As you reflect on the lessons in this section, remember that mastering life is not a one-time achievement—it's a lifelong journey. There will be times when you stray from your routines, struggle with boundaries, or feel overwhelmed by the demands of leadership. That's okay. What matters is your commitment to keep coming back to the principles that ground you.

Mastering life is about progress, not perfection. It's about creating a life that supports your growth, aligns with your values, and allows you to lead with energy and purpose. By simplifying, setting boundaries, building routines, prioritizing rest, and aligning with your values, you are creating a foundation for sustained leadership success.

As you move forward, give yourself grace. Celebrate your progress, learn from your challenges, and continue to refine the framework that supports your leadership and well-being. Mastering life is not about doing everything perfectly—it's about living intentionally and leading authentically.

Takeaway: Life and leadership are intertwined. By mastering your life, you create the conditions for effective, impactful leadership. Embrace the journey, and let your life be a reflection of your values, priorities, and purpose.

******

Next Steps to Implement Life Mastery Techniques

Mastering life is not about drastic, overnight changes; it's about adopting intentional habits and practices that align with your values, priorities, and vision. The journey to life mastery begins with small, consistent steps. These steps help you build a sustainable framework that supports your leadership, well-being, and long-term success.

Now that we've explored the principles of life mastery—simplifying your life, setting boundaries, creating routines, prioritizing play, and aligning with your values—it's time to focus on actionable ways to implement these techniques into your daily life. This chapter will guide you through the next steps to begin incorporating life mastery strategies so you can lead with clarity, purpose, and balance.

1. Assess Your Current Habits and Priorities

The first step in implementing life mastery techniques is to take an honest look at where you currently stand. Reflect on your daily habits, routines, and priorities. Are they aligned with your long-term goals and values? Are there areas where you feel overwhelmed or out of balance?

Use this self-assessment as a starting point for change. Ask yourself questions like:

- What activities or commitments are draining my energy?

- Which areas of my life feel cluttered or disorganized?

- Am I making enough time for rest, play, and meaningful relationships?

- Which habits are supporting my leadership, and which are holding me back?

Write down your reflections and identify one or two areas where you'd like to focus first. This clarity will help you create a targeted plan for implementing the strategies we've discussed.

2. Start Small: Focus on One Change at a Time

Life mastery is a marathon, not a sprint. Trying to overhaul your entire life at once can be overwhelming and unsustainable. Instead, focus on one change at a time. Choose one area—whether it's simplifying your schedule, setting a boundary, or creating a new routine—and commit to making consistent progress.

For example, if you struggle with saying no, start by identifying one area where you can set a clear boundary. Practice saying no in low-stakes situations and gradually build your confidence. Or, if you want to prioritize rest and play, begin by scheduling one leisure activity into your week. As you gain momentum in one area, you'll feel more empowered to tackle others.

The key is to start small and celebrate your progress along the way. Each step you take reinforces your commitment to life mastery and builds a foundation for sustained change.

3. Create a Simplification Plan

Simplifying your life is one of the most impactful techniques for achieving clarity and focus. To get started, create a plan to simplify one area of your life, such as your schedule, environment, or commitments.

- **Simplify Your Schedule**: Review your calendar and identify tasks or meetings that don't align with your priorities. Delegate, reschedule, or eliminate them to create more space for meaningful work and rest.

- **Declutter Your Environment**: Choose one area of your home or workspace to declutter. Clear out items that no longer serve you and organize your space in a way that feels peaceful and efficient.

- **Streamline Your Commitments**: Reflect on your commitments and decide which ones truly align with your values. Let go of any obligations that feel draining or unnecessary.

By simplifying one area at a time, you'll create a ripple effect of clarity and intention throughout your life.

4. Establish Boundaries and Communicate Them Clearly

Boundaries are essential for protecting your energy and time, but they only work if they're clear and consistently enforced. Begin by identifying one area where you need a boundary—whether it's work hours, personal time, or relationships—and create a plan for implementing it.

For example, if you want to protect your evenings for family time, set a specific end to your workday and communicate this boundary to your colleagues. Be clear and firm but also kind and professional. Practice reinforcing this boundary by politely declining after-hours work requests or turning off notifications during your personal time.

Remember, boundaries are a form of self-respect. The more you honor your boundaries, the more others will respect them as well.

5. Design a Routine That Supports Your Goals

Routines are powerful tools for creating stability and consistency in your life. To implement a productive routine, start by designing one that aligns with your goals and energy levels.

- **Morning Routine**: Create a morning ritual that sets the tone for your day. This might include journaling, meditating, exercising, or reviewing your priorities.

- **Workday Routine**: Use time-blocking to structure your workday. Schedule focused work periods for high-priority tasks and include time for breaks and reflection.

- **Evening Routine**: End your day with a calming routine that helps you unwind and reflect. This could involve reading, journaling, or preparing for the next day.

Test your routine for a few weeks and adjust as needed. The goal is to find a rhythm that feels natural and supports your productivity and well-being.

6. Schedule Time for Play and Rest

Rest and play are non-negotiable for life mastery. To ensure you prioritize downtime, schedule it into your calendar just as you would a work meeting or deadline. Treat this time as sacred—it's an investment in your energy, creativity, and resilience.

Choose leisure activities that genuinely recharge you, such as hiking, painting, or spending time with loved ones. Be intentional about disconnecting from work during these moments, and give yourself permission to fully enjoy them. The more you prioritize play and rest, the more energized and focused you'll be in your leadership.

7. Align Your Actions with Your Values

Life mastery is about living in alignment with your values. Take time to clarify what matters most to you—whether it's family, health, personal growth, or making a difference in the world. Use these values as a compass for your decisions and actions.

When faced with a decision, ask yourself: Does this align with my values? Does it move me closer to my goals? By consistently aligning your actions with your priorities, you'll create a life that feels purposeful and fulfilling.

8. Track Your Progress and Reflect Regularly

Implementing life mastery techniques is an ongoing process, and regular reflection is key to staying on track. Set aside time each week or month to review your progress. Reflect on questions like:

- What's working well in my life?

- Where do I feel out of balance or overwhelmed?

- What adjustments can I make to better align with my goals and values?

Use this reflection time to celebrate your wins and identify areas for growth. Life mastery isn't about perfection—it's about continuous improvement and intentional living.

Take the First Step Toward Mastery

The journey to mastering life is a deeply personal and empowering process. It's not about achieving a perfect balance or following a rigid formula—it's about creating a life that supports your growth, reflects your values, and empowers you to lead with clarity and purpose.

Start small. Choose one technique, implement it with intention, and build from there. Each step you take brings you closer to a life that is balanced, fulfilling, and aligned with your vision. Remember, mastery is not a destination—it's a journey. Embrace the process, trust in your progress, and know that every small step forward is a powerful act of leadership and self-care.

Part III
Master Your Business

Chapter 11

You Have to Give to Get Value

In the world of business, success is not just about profit margins, market share, or quarterly earnings. At its core, business is about value-creating it, delivering it, and ultimately, receiving it in return. As a leader, your influence and effectiveness are directly tied to how well you understand this fundamental truth: to get value, you must first give it. The businesses and leaders who thrive are those who prioritize serving others—whether it's their customers, employees, or community—and who consistently deliver solutions that meet real needs.

Creating and delivering value isn't just a strategy; it's a mindset. It requires you to think beyond transactions and focus on relationships, impact, and long-term outcomes. Whether you're leading a team, launching a product, or building a brand, the question at the heart of everything you do should be: How can I create value for others? When you lead with this question, success follows—not because you're chasing it, but because you're building something meaningful.

In this chapter, we'll explore the importance of creating and delivering value in business, why it's essential for sustainable success, and how you can adopt a value-driven approach to leadership that sets you apart.

What Does It Mean to Create Value?

Creating value means offering something that meets a need, solves a problem, or improves the lives of others. It's about providing more than just a product or service—it's about creating an experience, an outcome, or a solution that resonates with the people you serve. Value can take many forms: quality, innovation, convenience, trust, or emotional connection. Whatever the form, value is what makes people choose your business, stay loyal to your brand, and recommend you to others.

Think about some of the world's most successful companies—brands like Apple, Amazon, or Tesla. Their success isn't just about the products they sell; it's about the value they provide. Apple delivers sleek, intuitive technology that enhances the user experience. Amazon creates value through convenience, speed, and reliability. Tesla combines innovation with a mission to create a more sustainable future. These companies thrive because they focus on creating value that matters to their customers.

As a leader, your role is to ensure that value creation is at the heart of your business strategy. This means understanding the needs of your audience, anticipating their desires, and delivering solutions that exceed their expectations. When you make value your priority, you create a foundation for trust, loyalty, and long-term success.

The Give-First Mindset: Why You Must Give Before You Get

In business, it's easy to focus on what you want to achieve—whether it's higher profits, more market share, or greater influence. But, the most successful leaders and businesses understand that getting value always starts with giving it. This is the give-first mindset: the idea that by prioritizing others' needs, you ultimately create the conditions for your own success.

The give-first mindset is about building relationships before transactions. It's about asking yourself, "What can I offer?" instead of "What can I gain?" For example:

- **With Customers**: Instead of focusing solely on sales, focus on solving problems. Offer free resources, share knowledge, or provide exceptional customer service that goes above and beyond expectations.

- **With Employees**: Invest in your team's growth and well-being. Provide opportunities for professional development, foster a supportive culture, and show appreciation for their contributions.

- **With Partners**: Build trust by being transparent, reliable, and collaborative. Offer support, share insights, and create partnerships that are mutually beneficial.

The give-first mindset doesn't mean giving away your time, resources, or energy indiscriminately. It means being intentional about how you create value for others, knowing that when you give authentically, the returns will follow.

Value as the Foundation of Trust and Loyalty

Creating and delivering value is about more than just meeting immediate needs—it's about building trust and fostering loyalty. When people feel that you genuinely care about their success, they're more likely to support your business, stick with your brand, and advocate for you to others.

Trust is built when you consistently deliver on your promises and provide value that exceeds expectations. For example, if you run a business, it might mean delivering a product that's not only high-quality but also backed by exceptional customer service. If you're a leader, it might mean being transparent, reliable, and supportive so your team knows they can count on you.

Loyalty, on the other hand, comes from creating a deeper emotional connection with the people you serve. It's not just about what you offer— it's about how you make people feel. When your customers or employees feel valued, heard, and supported, they become your biggest advocates. They stay with you not because they have to but because they want to.

Creating value builds trust and loyalty that stand the test of time. It's what turns one-time customers into repeat buyers, employees into engaged team members, and business relationships into long-term partnerships.

Delivering Value in Every Interaction

One of the most powerful ways to lead with value is to make it a priority in every interaction. Whether you're speaking with a client, mentoring an employee, or negotiating a deal, ask yourself: How can I add value in this moment?

Here are some practical ways to deliver value in different contexts:

- **With Customers**: Listen actively to their needs and feedback. Offer personalized solutions that address their unique challenges. Surprise them with unexpected touches of care, like a handwritten thank-you note or a follow-up call to check on their satisfaction.

- **With Employees**: Provide clear communication, constructive feedback, and opportunities for growth. Celebrate their successes, support them during challenges, and show them that their work makes a difference.

- **With Stakeholders**: Be transparent, honest, and proactive in your communication. Share insights and data that help them make informed decisions. Focus on building win-win solutions that benefit everyone involved.

When you approach every interaction with the intention to create value, you elevate your leadership and strengthen your impact.

Sustaining Value Creation for Long-Term Success

Creating value isn't a one-time effort—it's a continuous process. The needs of your customers, employees, and stakeholders will evolve over time, and your ability to adapt and innovate is what will sustain your success.

To sustain value creation:

1. **Stay Curious**: Continuously seek to understand the changing needs and desires of the people you serve. Ask questions, gather feedback, and be open to new ideas.

2. **Innovate Constantly**: Don't settle for "good enough." Look for ways to improve your products, services, and processes. Innovation is a key driver of value and keeps your business relevant.

3. **Measure Impact**: Track the outcomes of your value-creation efforts. Whether it's customer satisfaction, employee engagement, or business growth, use data to understand what's working and where you can improve.

4. **Commit to Excellence**: Consistently strive to exceed expectations. Delivering exceptional value requires dedication, attention to detail, and a commitment to excellence in everything you do.

The Ripple Effect of Value Creation

When you focus on creating and delivering value, the benefits extend far beyond your immediate goals. The value you give creates a ripple effect, inspiring others to pay it forward. Your customers become loyal advocates, your employees become passionate contributors, and your business becomes a trusted partner in your industry.

The give-first mindset transforms not only your business but also your leadership. It shifts your focus from self-interest to service, from transactions to relationships, and from short-term gains to long-term impact. By leading with value, you create a legacy of trust, loyalty, and success that continues to grow over time.

Value is the Currency of Leadership

At its heart, business is about relationships. And in every relationship—whether with customers, employees, or stakeholders—value is the currency that drives trust, loyalty, and success. When you lead with the intention to give before you get, you create a foundation for sustainable growth and meaningful impact.

As you move forward, remember this simple truth: you have to give to get value. Focus on understanding the needs of the people you serve and commit to exceeding their expectations. When you make value your priority, you unlock the full potential of your leadership and your business.

******

Ways to Enhance Value Proposition to Stakeholders

Creating and delivering value is at the heart of business success, but maintaining that value over time requires continuous effort and innovation. Stakeholders—whether they are customers, employees, investors, or partners—are the lifeblood of your business, and ensuring your value proposition resonates with them is essential for long-term success.

A strong value proposition clearly communicates why someone should choose your business, invest in your vision, or align with your goals. It answers the critical question: *What's in it for them?* But to truly enhance your value proposition, you must go beyond meeting basic needs—you need to understand your stakeholders deeply and deliver solutions that exceed their expectations.

In this section, we'll explore actionable ways to refine and enhance your value proposition to strengthen relationships, build trust, and drive results.

1. Understand Stakeholder Needs and Pain Points

Enhancing your value proposition begins with understanding the people you're serving. Whether they are customers, employees, or investors, every stakeholder has unique needs, goals, and challenges. To deliver meaningful value, you must first identify what matters most to them.

- **Customers**: What problems are they trying to solve? What goals are they striving to achieve? What frustrates or excites them about the current solutions available in the market? Gathering insights through surveys, feedback, or direct conversations can help you understand how to better serve your customers.

- **Employees**: What motivates them to perform at their best? Are they seeking opportunities for growth, recognition for their contributions, or a healthier work-life balance? By understanding their needs, you can create an environment that inspires engagement and loyalty.

- **Investors**: What outcomes are they looking for? Are they focused on financial returns, social impact, or innovation? Understanding their priorities allows you to align your goals with theirs and build a compelling case for partnership.

Once you've identified stakeholder needs and pain points, use this information to shape your value proposition. The more specific and relevant your solutions, the more likely they are to resonate and drive results.

2. Offer Tailored Solutions

One-size-fits-all approaches rarely work when it comes to delivering value. To truly enhance your value proposition, you need to offer solutions that are tailored to the unique needs and preferences of each stakeholder group.

- **For Customers**: Personalization is key. Consider how you can customize your products, services, or experiences to meet individual customer needs. For example, a technology company might offer tiered service plans to cater to both budget-conscious customers and those seeking premium features. Tailored solutions show customers that you understand and care about their specific challenges.

- **For Employees**: Provide flexibility and opportunities for growth. This could mean offering personalized development plans, mentorship opportunities, or flexible work arrangements. Tailoring benefits and rewards to individual preferences demonstrates that you value each employee as a unique contributor.

- **For Investors**: Align your offerings with their priorities. If an investor is focused on sustainability, highlight your company's efforts to reduce environmental impact. If they're interested in financial growth, showcase your strategic roadmap for scaling and profitability.

By tailoring your solutions, you create a sense of connection and relevance that strengthens your relationships with stakeholders and sets your business apart from the competition.

3. Communicate Your Unique Value Clearly

A strong value proposition is only effective if stakeholders understand it. Clear communication is essential for helping stakeholders see the unique benefits your business offers. Your messaging should be concise, compelling, and focused on the outcomes that matter most to your audience.

- **Focus on Benefits, Not Features**: When describing your offerings, highlight the benefits stakeholders will gain rather than just listing features. For example, instead of saying, "Our software has a built-in analytics tool," explain, "Our software helps you make data-driven decisions faster, saving time and boosting efficiency."

- **Use Stories to Illustrate Impact**: Real-life examples and success stories are powerful tools for communicating value. Share testimonials, case studies, or before-and-after scenarios to show how your solutions have made a tangible difference for others.

- **Simplify Complex Concepts**: Avoid jargon or overly technical language. Make your value proposition easy to understand, even for those who may not be familiar with your industry.

Clear communication ensures that stakeholders not only understand your value but also see how it directly aligns with their goals.

4. Continuously Innovate and Improve

In a rapidly changing business landscape, standing still is not an option. To enhance your value proposition, you must continually innovate and adapt to meet evolving stakeholder needs. Innovation doesn't always mean creating something entirely new—it can also involve improving existing products, services, or processes.

- **For Customers**: Regularly update your offerings to reflect changing market trends and customer preferences. For example, if sustainability is becoming increasingly important to your audience, explore ways to make your products more eco-friendly.

- **For Employees**: Stay ahead of workplace trends by introducing new tools, resources, or initiatives that enhance the employee experience. This might include adopting cutting-edge collaboration software or launching wellness programs that support mental health.

- **For Investors**: Demonstrate a commitment to staying relevant by showcasing your ability to pivot, adapt, and seize new opportunities. Highlight your track record of innovation and your plans for future growth.

Innovation signals to stakeholders that you're forward-thinking, proactive, and committed to delivering the best possible value.

5. Build Emotional Connection

Value isn't just about practical benefits—it's also about emotional connection. Stakeholders are more likely to engage with and support businesses that align with their values, inspire trust, and make them feel valued.

- **For Customers**: Create experiences that evoke positive emotions. This might involve exceptional customer service, a seamless buying process, or a brand story that resonates on a personal level.

- **For Employees**: Foster a culture of recognition and appreciation. Celebrate milestones, acknowledge contributions, and create an environment where employees feel seen and valued.

- **For Investors**: Build trust by being transparent, reliable, and aligned with their values. Share your passion for your mission and vision, and show them that their support is making a meaningful impact.

When stakeholders feel an emotional connection to your business, they're more likely to stay loyal, advocate for your brand, and invest in your success.

6. Measure and Refine Your Value Proposition

To ensure your value proposition remains strong, it's important to regularly assess its effectiveness and make adjustments as needed. Use data and feedback to evaluate how well your offerings align with stakeholder needs and identify areas for improvement.

- **Gather Feedback**: Ask stakeholders for their input through surveys, interviews, or informal conversations. What do they value most about your business? What improvements would they like to see?

- **Analyze Metrics**: Track key performance indicators (KPIs) that reflect your value proposition's impact, such as customer retention, employee engagement, or investor satisfaction.

- **Iterate Based on Insights**: Use the insights you gather to refine your value proposition. Small adjustments, like enhancing a product feature or improving communication, can make a big difference in how stakeholders perceive your value.

Measuring and refining your value proposition ensures that it continues to resonate with stakeholders and adapt to changing circumstances.

Enhancing Value is an Ongoing Commitment

Enhancing your value proposition is not a one-time task—it's an ongoing commitment to understanding, serving, and exceeding the expectations of your stakeholders. By prioritizing their needs, tailoring your solutions, and continually innovating, you can strengthen your relationships, build trust, and create a competitive edge.

Remember, the best businesses don't just deliver value—they consistently enhance it. They listen to their stakeholders, adapt to their evolving needs, and go the extra mile to make a meaningful impact. When you lead with a focus on creating and delivering value, you not only achieve business success—you inspire loyalty, trust, and long-term growth.

Chapter 12

Selling is Serving

For many people, the word "sales" conjures images of pushy tactics, relentless pitches, and high-pressure techniques. It can feel transactional, uncomfortable, and impersonal. But what if we could reframe the way we think about sales? What if selling wasn't about convincing or coercing but about serving?

At its core, selling is not about manipulation or persuasion—it's about helping people. It's about identifying their needs, understanding their challenges, and offering solutions that genuinely improve their lives. When you approach sales with this service-driven mindset, it transforms the process from something transactional into something deeply relational and meaningful. Selling becomes an act of care, an opportunity to make a positive difference.

In this chapter, we'll explore how to reframe your sales strategies under the service paradigm. By adopting a service-driven approach to selling, you can build trust, create long-term relationships, and deliver value in a way that feels authentic and impactful—for both you and those you serve.

The Mindset Shift: From Selling to Serving

The first step in reframing your sales strategy is changing the way you think about sales. Instead of viewing sales as a way to meet your business goals, see it as an opportunity to serve others. When you approach sales with a service mindset, your focus shifts from "How can I close this deal?" to "How can I help this person?"

A service-driven sales mindset is rooted in:

- **Empathy**: Taking the time to understand your customer's needs, desires, and challenges.

- **Integrity**: Offering solutions that genuinely align with what the customer values and needs, not just what benefits you.

- **Collaboration**: Working with your customers to co-create solutions that meet their goals.

This mindset doesn't mean you stop caring about results or revenue—it means you achieve those outcomes by putting the customer's needs first. When customers feel that you're truly invested in their success, they're more likely to trust you, engage with your offerings, and become loyal advocates for your business.

Listening: The Foundation of Service-Driven Sales

One of the most important skills in service-driven sales is the ability to listen. Too often, salespeople focus on what they want to say rather than truly hearing what the customer is saying. But if you want to serve your customers effectively, you must first understand their needs—and that starts with active listening.

When you're in a sales conversation, focus on listening more than you talk. Ask open-ended questions that encourage your customer to share their challenges, goals, and concerns. For example:

- "What challenges are you currently facing in this area?"

- "What would success look like for you?"

- "What have you tried in the past, and what worked or didn't work?"

As you listen, pay attention not just to their words but also to their tone, body language, and emotions. These cues can provide valuable insights into their priorities and pain points. Resist the urge to jump in with a solution too quickly—take the time to fully understand their perspective first.

When customers feel heard and understood, they're more likely to trust you and see you as a partner in solving their problems rather than just someone trying to sell them something.

Aligning Solutions with Customer Needs

Once you've listened to your customer and gained a deep understanding of their needs, the next step is to align your solutions with those needs. This is where the service-driven approach really shines. Instead of trying to "sell" a product or service, you're offering something that genuinely addresses their challenges and helps them achieve their goals.

Start by clearly articulating how your solution meets their specific needs. Use their own words and concerns to frame your response. For example, instead of saying, "Our software is the most advanced on the market," you might say, "Based on what you shared about needing a simpler way to manage your team's workload, our software can help streamline those processes and free up more time for strategic planning."

Be honest about what your solution can and cannot do. If there are limitations, acknowledge them and focus on the areas where your offering provides the most value. Transparency builds trust and ensures that your customer feels confident in their decision.

If your solution isn't the right fit, don't be afraid to say so. Refer the customer to a resource or alternative that might be better suited to their needs. While this may seem counterintuitive, it reinforces your commitment to serving them authentically—and they're more likely to think of you positively in the future.

Building Relationships, Not Transactions

Service-driven sales is not about closing a deal and moving on—it's about building lasting relationships. Customers who feel cared for and supported are more likely to return, recommend your business to others, and become long-term partners in your success.

To build strong relationships:

- **Follow Up Thoughtfully**: After an initial conversation or sale, follow up with your customer to see how they're doing. Ask if they have questions, need additional support, or want to share feedback. This shows that you're invested in their ongoing success.

- **Add Value Beyond the Sale**: Share resources, insights, or tips that might benefit your customer, even if they're not directly related to the product or service you sold. For example, if you're a consultant, you might send them an article on industry trends that align with their goals.

- **Stay in Touch**: Relationships require ongoing care. Check-in with your customers periodically, even when you're not actively selling to them. A simple "How's everything going?" email or a quick call can go a long way in maintaining a strong connection.

When you focus on building relationships rather than just closing deals, you create a network of loyal customers who trust you and are eager to support your business.

Overcoming Objections with Empathy and Confidence

Every sales conversation comes with its own set of challenges, and objections are a natural part of the process. The service-driven approach to handling objections is rooted in empathy and confidence. Instead of seeing objections as obstacles, view them as opportunities to better understand your customer's concerns and provide clarity.

Here's how to approach objections:

1. **Acknowledge Their Concerns**: Start by validating their perspective. For example, if a customer says, "This seems too expensive," respond with, "I understand that cost is an important factor."

2. **Explore the Objection**: Ask open-ended questions to uncover the root of their concern. For example, "Can you tell me more about your budget priorities?" or "What specific value would make this investment worthwhile for you?"

3. **Provide Reassurance**: Address their concerns with clear, honest information. Focus on the benefits and outcomes they'll gain from your solution, using real-world examples or testimonials to illustrate your point.

4. **Offer Flexibility**: If appropriate, explore ways to customize your solution to better fit their needs. For example, you might offer a phased approach, a payment plan, or additional support.

By handling objections with empathy and confidence, you demonstrate that you're not just trying to sell—you're genuinely invested in finding the best solution for your customer.

Selling as an Act of Leadership

When you adopt the service-driven approach to sales, you're not just a salesperson—you're a leader. You're guiding your customers toward solutions that improve their lives, helping them overcome challenges, and empowering them to achieve their goals. Selling becomes an opportunity to lead with integrity, empathy, and purpose.

This mindset not only transforms the way you approach sales but it also enhances your influence and effectiveness as a leader. By focusing on service, you build trust, foster loyalty, and create lasting impact in every interaction.

Selling with Purpose

Reframing sales as an act of service changes everything. It shifts the focus from pushing products to providing solutions, from closing deals to building relationships, and from self-interest to shared success. When you approach sales with a service-driven mindset, you create value for your customers, build trust in your business, and set the foundation for sustainable success.

Remember, selling is not about convincing—it's about caring. By prioritizing the needs of those you serve, you not only elevate your sales strategies but also embody the true essence of leadership. In every sales conversation, ask yourself: *How can I help?* When you lead with this question, you'll find that selling becomes one of the most meaningful ways to make a difference.

******

Techniques for Ethical Selling That Builds Lasting Customer Relationships

Ethical selling isn't just about doing the right thing—it's about building trust, credibility, and long-term relationships with your customers. When you approach sales with integrity, you demonstrate respect for your customers' needs and priorities, creating a foundation for loyalty and mutual respect. Ethical selling ensures that your success is not achieved at the expense of others but through a shared sense of value and collaboration.

Customers are increasingly savvy and values-driven. They want to work with businesses and leaders who are transparent, honest, and committed to their well-being. By adopting ethical sales techniques, you not only differentiate yourself in a competitive market but also create a reputation that inspires trust and fosters lasting connections.

In this section, we'll explore practical techniques for ethical selling, providing you with tools to serve your customers with honesty, empathy, and care while strengthening your relationships and reputation.

1. Practice Transparency in All Interactions

Honesty is the cornerstone of ethical selling. Customers need to trust that the information you provide is accurate, complete, and free of misleading claims. Transparency not only builds credibility but also helps customers feel confident in their decisions.

- **Be Honest About Your Offerings**: Clearly communicate what your product or service can and cannot do. If there are limitations, be upfront about them. For example, if your solution works best for small teams but may not scale easily for large organizations, make that clear from the outset.

- **Avoid Overpromising**: Resist the temptation to exaggerate benefits or make guarantees you can't keep. Instead, focus on delivering realistic expectations and outlining the specific outcomes your customers can achieve.

- **Provide Full Disclosure**: If there are terms, fees, or conditions associated with your offering, share them early in the sales process. This eliminates surprises and ensures that your customers fully understand what they're agreeing to.

Transparency fosters trust, demonstrating that you prioritize your customers' needs over making a quick sale.

2. Prioritize Understanding Over Selling

Ethical selling starts with empathy and a genuine desire to understand your customers' needs, goals, and concerns. When you prioritize understanding over pitching, you create a space for meaningful conversations that lead to better solutions and stronger relationships.

- **Ask Thoughtful Questions**: Use open-ended questions to uncover your customers' pain points and aspirations. For example, "What challenges are you hoping to solve?" or "What does success look like for your team?"

- **Listen Actively**: Pay attention to what your customers are saying without interrupting or rushing to offer a solution. Show that you value their input by summarizing their concerns and asking clarifying questions.

- **Put Their Needs First**: Shift your mindset from "How can I sell this?" to "How can I help them?" This approach ensures that your recommendations are aligned with what's best for the customer, even if it means recommending an alternative solution.

When customers feel heard and understood, they're more likely to trust your guidance and see you as a partner in achieving their goals.

3. Provide Tailored Solutions

Ethical selling is about offering solutions that genuinely address your customers' unique needs. Avoid taking a one-size-fits-all approach, and instead, focus on customizing your recommendations to align with their specific goals and challenges.

- **Understand the Context**: Every customer's situation is different. Take the time to learn about their industry, company, and pain points before presenting a solution.

- **Highlight Relevant Features**: Focus on the aspects of your product or service that are most beneficial to your customer. For example, if a client is concerned about efficiency, emphasize how your solution saves time or simplifies processes.

- **Be Selective in Your Recommendations**: Offer only what you truly believe will add value. If your product or service isn't the best fit, be honest about it and suggest an alternative that better meets their needs.

By tailoring your approach, you demonstrate that you're invested in your customers' success, not just in making a sale.

4. Build Long-Term Relationships, Not Quick Wins

The goal of ethical selling is not to close a deal—it's to build lasting relationships based on trust and mutual benefit. This requires a commitment to your customers' long-term success, even after the sale is complete.

- **Follow Through on Promises**: Ensure that you deliver on everything you've promised during the sales process. If there are delays or issues, communicate them proactively and work to resolve them quickly.

- **Check In Regularly**: Stay connected with your customers after the sale. Ask for feedback, offer ongoing support, and show genuine interest in their progress. For example, a follow-up email or call to ask, "How's everything working out for you?" can go a long way in maintaining the relationship.

- **Add Value Beyond the Sale**: Share resources, insights, or updates that align with your customers' goals. For example, if you come across an industry trend or best practice that's relevant to their work, share it with them as a helpful resource.

When you focus on nurturing relationships rather than chasing short-term gains, you create a loyal customer base that trusts and values your partnership.

5. Respect the Customer's Decision-Making Process

Ethical selling means respecting your customers' autonomy and giving them the space to make informed decisions. High-pressure tactics and aggressive follow-ups can erode trust and damage your relationship.

- **Avoid Manipulative Techniques**: Refrain from using fear-based tactics, false urgency, or other manipulative strategies to push a sale. Instead, focus on providing the information and support your customers need to feel confident in their decision.

- **Be Patient**: Recognize that decision-making takes time. Allow your customers to ask questions, consult with their team, or explore other options without feeling rushed.

- **Empower Them with Knowledge**: Provide clear, comprehensive information about your offering, including pricing, benefits, and potential limitations. This ensures that they can make a well-informed choice.

When customers feel respected and empowered, they're more likely to view you as a trusted advisor and return to you for future needs.

6. Be Transparent About Your Motivations

Ethical selling doesn't mean hiding the fact that you have business goals—it means being transparent about your motivations while ensuring they align with the customer's best interests.

For example, you might say:

Our goal is to help businesses like yours streamline operations and improve efficiency. Based on what you've shared, I believe our solution can help you achieve those goals. Let me walk you through how it works."

This approach builds trust by showing that your motivations are aligned with their success, not just your bottom line.

7. Commit to Continuous Learning and Improvement

The landscape of ethical selling is always evolving, and staying committed to learning ensures that you're consistently providing the best possible service to your customers.

- **Seek Feedback**: Ask your customers for honest feedback about their experience with your sales process. Use their insights to identify areas for improvement.

- **Stay Informed**: Keep up with industry trends, customer preferences, and best practices in ethical selling. This knowledge allows you to adapt and stay relevant.

- **Reflect on Your Practices**: Regularly evaluate your sales techniques to ensure they align with your values and the needs of your customers. Ask yourself, "Am I serving my customers in the best way possible?"

Continuous improvement ensures that you're always striving to build trust, deliver value, and foster lasting relationships.

Selling with Integrity

Ethical selling isn't just good for your customers—it's good for your business. By prioritizing honesty, empathy, and respect in every sales interaction, you build a reputation for integrity that attracts loyal customers and inspires trust. Ethical selling transforms the sales process into a partnership where both you and your customers succeed.

When you lead with these techniques—transparency, empathy, tailored solutions, and a commitment to long-term relationships—you create a sales strategy that aligns with your values and strengthens your leadership. Remember, selling is serving, and every sale is an opportunity to make a meaningful impact on the lives of those you serve.

Chapter 13

Get Your Money Up

Money is often seen as a measure of success, but it's so much more than that—it's a tool. When managed wisely, money has the power to create opportunities, provide security, and drive both personal and business growth. For leaders, financial literacy is not just a skill; it's a necessity. Whether you're managing your personal finances, overseeing a business budget, or making strategic investments, your ability to understand and handle money effectively can determine your long-term success.

The truth is many talented and driven leaders fall short not because they lack vision or work ethic but because they don't have a strong grasp on financial management. But the good news is that financial literacy isn't about being a math genius or having a degree in economics—it's about understanding the basics, making informed decisions, and creating systems that support your goals.

In this chapter, we'll dive into the fundamentals of financial literacy and management. You'll learn how to master your personal and business finances, avoid common pitfalls, and create a financial foundation that empowers you to grow, lead, and thrive.

Why Financial Literacy Matters for Leaders

As a leader, your financial decisions have a ripple effect. They impact your ability to pursue opportunities, support your team, and achieve your goals. Yet, financial literacy is often overlooked as a cornerstone of effective leadership. Many leaders focus on vision and strategy but neglect to build the financial acumen needed to turn those ideas into sustainable success.

Financial literacy is about more than just balancing a budget or saving for the future—it's about understanding how money works and how to use it as a tool for growth. It's about knowing the difference between good debt and bad debt, understanding cash flow, and being able to interpret financial statements. It's also about cultivating the confidence to make informed decisions, whether you're negotiating a business deal, planning an investment, or managing your personal expenses.

When you have a strong foundation in financial literacy, you're better equipped to:

- Make strategic decisions that align with your goals.

- Build a business or personal budget that supports long-term growth.

- Navigate challenges like economic downturns or unexpected expenses.

- Spot opportunities for investment, growth, and innovation.

Simply put, financial literacy gives you the knowledge and tools you need to lead with clarity and confidence.

Mastering Personal Financial Management

Your personal finances are the foundation of your overall financial health. If you're not managing your personal money effectively, it can create stress, limit your opportunities, and undermine your ability to lead. The first step to getting your money up is taking control of your personal financial situation.

Here are some key principles of personal financial management:

1. **Create a Budget**: A budget is your roadmap for managing income, expenses, and savings. Start by tracking your spending to understand where your money is going. Then, categorize your expenses into essentials (like housing and groceries), discretionary spending (like dining out), and savings. Aim to allocate a portion of your income to saving and investing each month.

2. **Build an Emergency Fund**: Life is unpredictable, and having an emergency fund can protect you from financial setbacks. Aim to save three to six months' worth of living expenses in a separate account. This cushion provides peace of mind and flexibility in case of unexpected events like job loss, medical expenses, or major repairs.

3. **Pay Down Debt Strategically**: Not all debt is created equal. High-interest debt, like credit cards, should be prioritized for repayment, while low-interest debt, like a mortgage, can be managed over time. Use strategies like the debt snowball or debt avalanche method to tackle your balances and free up more money for savings and investments.

4. **Invest for the Future**: Saving is important, but investing is how you grow your wealth over time. Learn the basics of investing in stocks, bonds, and mutual funds, and consider working with a financial advisor to build a portfolio that aligns with your goals and risk tolerance.

5. **Protect Your Assets**: Financial security also means safeguarding what you've built. Ensure you have adequate insurance (health, life, property) and create a will or estate plan to protect your family and assets.

When you take control of your personal finances, you create a strong foundation that supports your leadership and enables you to seize new opportunities.

Financial Management for Business Growth

For leaders in business, financial literacy is even more critical. The health of your organization depends on your ability to manage budgets, control cash flow, and make strategic investments. Whether you're leading a small team or running a multimillion-dollar enterprise, understanding the financial side of your business is essential.

Here are the key components of financial management for business growth:

1. **Understand Cash Flow**: Cash flow is the lifeblood of your business. It's not just about how much money you're making—it's about when and how that money comes in and goes out. Track your cash flow regularly to ensure you have enough liquidity to cover expenses and invest in growth.

2. **Create and Stick to a Budget**: A business budget helps you allocate resources effectively and avoid overspending. Break your budget into categories like operational expenses, marketing, payroll, and R&D. Monitor your spending to ensure it aligns with your goals.

3. **Know Your Financial Metrics**: As a leader, you should be familiar with key financial metrics that indicate the health of your business. These include profit margins, revenue growth, return on investment (ROI), and customer acquisition costs (CAC). Use these metrics to make informed decisions and identify areas for improvement.

4. **Leverage Good Debt**: In business, not all debt is bad. Loans or credit can be strategic tools for growth when used wisely. For example, taking out a loan to invest in new equipment or hire additional staff can help you scale your business. The key is to ensure that the debt will generate returns that outweigh the costs.

5. **Plan for the Long Term**: Growth isn't just about today—it's about building a sustainable future. Create a financial plan that outlines

your long-term goals and the steps you'll take to achieve them. This might include saving for expansion, investing in technology, or building a reserve fund for lean times.

Common Financial Pitfalls to Avoid

As you work to improve your financial literacy, it's important to be aware of common pitfalls that can derail your progress. Here are some mistakes to watch out for:

- **Ignoring the Numbers**: Financial reports and data might seem intimidating, but ignoring them can lead to poor decisions. Take the time to learn how to read financial statements and analyze key metrics.

- **Overextending Your Budget**: It's easy to get caught up in the excitement of growth, but overspending can put your personal or business finances at risk. Stick to your budget and make strategic, incremental investments.

- **Failing to Diversify**: Whether it's your personal investments or your business revenue streams, relying too heavily on one source can be risky. Diversify to protect yourself from unexpected changes.

- **Neglecting Tax Planning**: Taxes are a major expense for both individuals and businesses. Work with a tax professional to ensure you're taking advantage of deductions, credits, and strategies that minimize your tax liability.

Cultivating a Growth Mindset Around Money

Finally, getting your money up requires adopting a growth mindset around finances. This means viewing money not as a source of stress but as a tool for creating opportunities and achieving your goals. Commit to learning, stay curious, and don't be afraid to ask for help when needed.

- **Educate Yourself**: Read books, take courses, and seek advice from financial experts to deepen your understanding of money management.

- **Stay Open to Feedback**: If you make a financial mistake, view it as a learning opportunity. Reflect on what went wrong and how you can improve in the future.

- **Celebrate Small Wins**: Every step you take toward financial mastery—whether it's paying off a credit card or hitting a revenue target—deserves to be celebrated. These wins build momentum and keep you motivated.

Lead with Financial Confidence

Mastering financial literacy and management is a game-changer for both personal and business growth. When you understand how to manage money effectively, you gain the power to make informed decisions, seize opportunities, and lead with confidence.

Remember, financial success isn't about luck—it's about strategy, discipline, and a willingness to learn. By prioritizing financial literacy, you're not just setting yourself up for success—you're building a foundation that empowers you to lead, inspire, and create lasting impact. So, take the first step, get your money up, and watch how it transforms every area of your life and leadership.

******

Investment Strategies and Financial Planning Tips

Growing your wealth and securing your financial future requires more than just saving money—it calls for smart investments and a solid financial plan. Investing is one of the most powerful tools for building wealth over time, but it can feel intimidating, especially if you're new to it. The good news is that you don't need to be a financial wizard to succeed. With a clear strategy, the right mindset, and consistent effort, anyone can use investments to achieve their goals.

In this section, we'll explore practical investment strategies and financial planning tips that will help you take control of your financial future. Whether you're focused on personal wealth-building or managing the finances of your business, these principles will empower you to make informed decisions and maximize your returns.

1. Start with Clear Goals

Every successful investment strategy begins with a clear understanding of what you want to achieve. Your financial goals act as a roadmap, guiding your investment decisions and helping you stay focused.

- **Short-Term Goals**: These might include building an emergency fund, saving for a vacation, or funding a business expansion. For short-term goals, prioritize low-risk investments, such as high-yield savings accounts or certificates of deposit (CDs), that provide stability and liquidity.

- **Long-Term Goals**: These include retirement, buying a home, or creating generational wealth. For long-term goals, you can take on more risk by investing in stocks, mutual funds, or real estate, as these assets typically offer higher returns over time.

Be specific about your goals. Instead of saying, "I want to save more money," say, "I want to save $50,000 for a down payment on a house within five years." Clear goals make it easier to create a focused investment strategy.

2. Diversify Your Portfolio

One of the golden rules of investing is diversification. Putting all your money into a single asset or sector is risky because you're relying entirely on its success. Diversifying your investments spreads that risk and increases the likelihood of steady returns.

Here's how to diversify effectively:

- **Asset Classes**: Invest in a mix of stocks, bonds, real estate, and cash equivalents. Each asset class performs differently depending on market conditions, so diversification helps balance your portfolio.

- **Industries and Sectors**: Within the stock market, invest in a variety of industries—such as technology, healthcare, and consumer goods—to reduce the impact of poor performance in any one sector.

- **Geography**: Consider including international investments in your portfolio to take advantage of global growth opportunities and reduce exposure to local market risks.

Diversification doesn't guarantee profits, but it does reduce the risk of significant losses, providing a more stable foundation for long-term growth.

3. Understand Risk and Return

Every investment carries some level of risk, and the potential return is often directly tied to that risk. Understanding your risk tolerance—the amount of risk you're comfortable taking—is essential for creating an investment strategy that works for you.

- **Low-Risk Investments**: These include bonds, savings accounts, and money market funds. While they offer lower returns, they provide stability and are ideal for short-term goals or risk-averse investors.

- **Moderate-Risk Investments**: Mutual funds, ETFs (exchange-traded funds), and dividend-paying stocks fall into this category. They offer a balance between risk and return, making them suitable for medium- to long-term goals.

- **High-Risk Investments**: Individual stocks, cryptocurrencies, and startups carry higher risks but also the potential for significant returns. These are best for investors with a high tolerance for risk and a long investment horizon.

Before making any investment, evaluate its risk level and ask yourself if it aligns with your financial goals and risk tolerance.

4. Invest Consistently

The most successful investors aren't those who time the market perfectly—they're the ones who invest consistently over time. This approach, known as dollar-cost averaging, involves investing a fixed amount of money at regular intervals, regardless of market conditions.

- **Why It Works**: Dollar-cost averaging reduces the impact of market volatility. When prices are high, your fixed investment buys fewer shares; when prices are low, it buys more shares. Over time, this strategy helps you avoid the pitfalls of emotional investing.

- **How to Do It**: Set up automatic contributions to your investment accounts, such as a retirement plan or brokerage account. Treat these contributions as non-negotiable, just like paying your bills.

Consistent investing builds discipline and ensures that you're steadily growing your wealth, even during periods of market uncertainty.

5. Take Advantage of Tax-Advantaged Accounts

Taxes can take a significant bite out of your investment returns, but with the right strategies, you can minimize your tax burden and keep more of your money working for you. One of the best ways to do this is by using tax-advantaged accounts.

- **Retirement Accounts**: Contribute to accounts like 401(k)s, IRAs, or Roth IRAs. These accounts offer tax benefits, such as tax-deferred growth or tax-free withdrawals in retirement, depending on the type of account.

- **Health Savings Accounts (HSAs)**: If you have a high-deductible health plan, an HSA allows you to save for medical expenses with triple tax advantages: contributions are tax-deductible, earnings grow tax-free, and withdrawals for qualified expenses are tax-free.

- **529 Plans**: For education savings, 529 plans provide tax-free growth and withdrawals when funds are used for qualified education expenses.

Using these accounts strategically can help you grow your investments while reducing your tax liability.

6. Seek Professional Advice

If you're unsure where to start or feel overwhelmed by the complexities of investing, don't hesitate to seek professional advice. A financial advisor can help you create a customized investment plan that aligns with your goals, risk tolerance, and timeline.

- **How to Choose an Advisor**: Look for a fiduciary advisor, meaning they're legally obligated to act in your best interest. Ask about their qualifications, fees, and approach to investing.

- **What to Expect**: A good financial advisor will help you clarify your goals, create a diversified portfolio, and adjust your strategy as your needs evolve. They can also provide guidance during market downturns, helping you stay focused on the long term.

While professional advice comes at a cost, it can save you time, reduce stress, and potentially improve your investment outcomes.

7. Plan for the Unexpected

No matter how well you plan, life is full of surprises. Building a financial safety net ensures that you're prepared for the unexpected while staying on track with your investment goals.

- **Emergency Fund**: Keep three to six months' worth of living expenses in a liquid, easily accessible account. This fund provides a buffer in case of job loss, medical emergencies, or unexpected expenses.

- **Insurance**: Protect yourself and your loved ones with adequate insurance coverage, including health, life, disability, and property insurance.

- **Diversified Income Streams**: Explore ways to diversify your income, such as rental properties, side businesses, or dividend-paying investments. This reduces your reliance on a single source of income and provides greater financial stability.

Planning for the unexpected allows you to navigate challenges with confidence and minimize disruptions to your investment strategy.

Build Wealth with Purpose

Investment strategies and financial planning are about more than just accumulating wealth—they're about creating opportunities, achieving your goals, and building a secure future for yourself and those you care about. By setting clear goals, diversifying your portfolio, and investing consistently, you can harness the power of compound growth and make your money work for you.

Remember, investing is a long-term journey. It requires patience, discipline, and a willingness to adapt as circumstances change. With the right strategies and mindset, you can take control of your financial future and create a legacy of growth, stability, and success.

Chapter 14

Don't Be Afraid to Ask for Help

One of the greatest myths in leadership and business is the idea that success is a solo journey. We often admire stories of self-made individuals, imagining them as lone warriors who climbed to the top on their own. But if you dig deeper into any success story, you'll find that behind every great leader, entrepreneur, or innovator is a network of mentors, advisors, and supporters who played a critical role in their journey.

Asking for help is not a sign of weakness—it's a mark of wisdom and strength. It's an acknowledgment that no one knows everything and that the right guidance, advice, and connections can accelerate your growth and help you navigate challenges with confidence. Whether you're building a business, leading a team, or striving for personal growth, surrounding yourself with the right people can make all the difference.

In this chapter, we'll explore the power of mentorship and networks in business advancement. You'll learn why it's essential to seek help, how to build meaningful relationships with mentors and peers, and how to leverage these connections to unlock opportunities and reach new heights.

The Role of Mentorship in Success

A mentor is someone who has walked the path before you, someone who can provide guidance, share insights, and help you avoid common pitfalls. The value of mentorship lies in its ability to fast-track your growth by giving you access to the wisdom and experience of those who've already achieved what you're striving for.

Mentors can help you in several ways:

- **Providing Clarity**: A mentor can help you see the bigger picture, prioritize your goals, and make decisions with confidence.

- **Offering Perspective**: When you're stuck in the weeds of a problem, a mentor can offer a fresh perspective and help you find solutions you might not have considered.

- **Sharing Lessons Learned**: Mentors can share their successes and failures, giving you valuable insights into what works and what doesn't.

- **Building Confidence**: Having someone in your corner who believes in your potential can boost your self-confidence and motivate you to take bold steps.

Whether it's a seasoned professional in your field, a successful entrepreneur, or someone whose leadership style you admire, the right mentor can become an invaluable partner in your journey.

Finding the Right Mentor

Finding the right mentor requires intention and effort. The goal is to connect with someone whose experience, values, and perspective align with your goals. Here are some tips for finding a mentor:

1. **Define What You Need**: Be clear about what you're looking for in a mentor. Are you seeking industry-specific expertise, leadership advice, or help navigating a particular challenge? Knowing your needs will help you identify the right person.

2. **Look for Alignment**: Choose someone whose values and approach resonate with you. A mentor-mentee relationship works best when there's mutual respect and shared principles.

3. **Expand Your Search**: Don't limit yourself to your immediate circle. Attend industry events, join professional organizations, or use platforms like LinkedIn to connect with potential mentors.

4. **Make the Ask Thoughtfully**: When reaching out to a potential mentor, be respectful of their time. Clearly articulate why you admire them, what you hope to learn, and how you envision the mentorship relationship.

Remember, mentorship is a two-way street. While your mentor will guide and support you, it's important to show appreciation, follow through on their advice, and demonstrate your commitment to personal and professional growth.

The Value of Building a Strong Network

While mentorship is a one-on-one relationship, your network is a broader web of connections that can open doors, provide resources, and offer support. A strong network is essential for business advancement because it connects you to people who can help you find opportunities, solve problems, and grow.

Your network might include:

- **Peers**: Colleagues and professionals at a similar stage in their careers who can offer advice, share experiences, and collaborate on projects.

- **Industry Leaders**: Influential figures in your field who can provide insights, trends, and strategic advice.

- **Cross-Industry Connections**: People from different industries or disciplines who can offer fresh perspectives and help you think outside the box.

- **Supportive Allies**: Friends, family, and advocates who believe in your potential and offer encouragement.

The key to building a strong network is to focus on relationships, not transactions. Networking isn't about collecting business cards or adding connections on LinkedIn—it's about creating genuine, meaningful connections based on trust, respect, and mutual benefit.

******

How to Seek Out and Engage with Mentors Effectively

Finding the right mentor can be transformative, offering guidance, insights, and encouragement that propel you toward your goals. But mentorship isn't something that happens by chance—it requires intention, effort, and mutual commitment. A successful mentoring relationship is built on trust, respect, and clear communication, and it begins with knowing how to approach potential mentors and engage with them effectively.

In this section, we'll explore actionable strategies for seeking out mentors and building meaningful, productive relationships that support your growth and success.

1. Define Your Goals and Needs

Before reaching out to a potential mentor, take time to reflect on what you're hoping to achieve. Understanding your goals and the specific areas where you need guidance will help you identify the right mentor and communicate your needs clearly.

- **Identify Your Goals**: Are you looking to improve your leadership skills, navigate a career transition, or learn about a specific industry? Having a clear purpose for seeking mentorship will make it easier to find someone whose expertise aligns with your aspirations.

- **Pinpoint Your Challenges**: Think about the obstacles you're facing or the skills you want to develop. For example, you might need help with strategic decision-making, team management, or personal branding.

- **Consider Your Ideal Mentor**: Reflect on the qualities, experience, or background you're looking for in a mentor. Do you want someone who has been in your industry for decades, or are you seeking a peer mentor who can relate to your current stage of growth?

By clarifying your needs, you'll be better equipped to seek out a mentor who can provide the right guidance.

2. Identify Potential Mentors

Once you've defined your goals, the next step is to identify potential mentors who align with your needs. A mentor doesn't have to be a celebrity in your field—they just need to have the experience, perspective, and willingness to support your growth.

Here are some places to look for potential mentors:

- **Professional Networks**: Reach out to colleagues, industry contacts, or members of professional organizations. Networking events and conferences are great places to meet experienced professionals who may be open to mentorship.

- **Workplace**: If you're employed, look within your organization. Senior leaders, managers, or colleagues in other departments may be willing to mentor you.

- **Online Communities**: Platforms like LinkedIn, industry forums, or social media groups can connect you with professionals who share your interests or goals.

- **Friends and Family Connections**: Don't overlook your personal network. Friends, relatives, or acquaintances may know someone who would be an excellent mentor for you.

- **Alumni Networks**: If you're a college or university graduate, your school's alumni network can be a valuable resource for finding mentors who understand your background.

Keep an open mind—sometimes, the best mentors are people you wouldn't have initially considered.

3. Make the Ask Thoughtfully

Approaching a potential mentor can feel intimidating, but it doesn't have to be. The key is to be genuine, respectful, and clear about your intentions. Here's how to make a strong first impression when asking someone to be your mentor:

- **Do Your Research**: Learn about the person's background, career, and areas of expertise. This shows that you've put thought into why you're approaching them specifically.

- **Start with a Conversation**: Instead of immediately asking for a long-term commitment, request a brief meeting or phone call to discuss your goals and seek their advice. This gives both of you a chance to see if the relationship is a good fit.

- **Be Specific and Respectful**: When making the ask, explain why you admire their work and what you hope to gain from their mentorship. For example: "I've followed your career in [industry] and admire your success in [specific achievement]. I'm currently working on [specific goal] and would love to learn from your experience. Would you be open to meeting for coffee or a quick call to discuss this?"

- **Keep It Flexible**: Acknowledge their time constraints and let them know you're willing to work around their schedule. Show that you value their time and are committed to making the relationship productive.

Not everyone will say yes, and that's okay. Be gracious regardless of their response, and continue seeking out others who align with your goals.

4. Set Clear Expectations

Once you've connected with a mentor, it's important to establish a foundation for a successful relationship by setting clear expectations. This ensures that both you and your mentor are aligned and understand how to make the most of your time together.

- **Define the Purpose**: Be clear about what you're hoping to achieve through the mentorship. For example, are you looking for guidance on a specific project, career advice, or ongoing support for personal growth?

- **Agree on the Format**: Decide how often you'll meet and the best way to communicate. Will you have in-person meetings, video calls, or email check-ins? Setting a regular schedule helps maintain momentum.

- **Set Goals Together**: Work with your mentor to outline specific, measurable goals for your mentorship. This gives the relationship structure and ensures that your time together is focused and productive.

- **Establish Boundaries**: Be mindful of your mentor's time and commitments. Avoid overloading them with requests, and respect any boundaries they set around availability or topics of discussion.

By setting clear expectations upfront, you create a framework for a mentoring relationship that is purposeful and mutually beneficial.

5. Engage Actively and Show Gratitude

A mentorship is not a one-way street—it's a partnership. To make the most of the relationship, you need to be an active participant and show genuine appreciation for your mentor's time and guidance.

- **Be Prepared**: Come to each meeting with specific questions, updates, or topics to discuss. This shows that you're taking the mentorship seriously and value their input.

- **Take Initiative**: Follow through on the advice and action steps your mentor suggests. Demonstrating your commitment to growth reinforces their investment in you.

- **Express Gratitude**: Regularly thank your mentor for their time, insights, and support. A handwritten note, a thoughtful message, or a public acknowledgment can go a long way in showing your appreciation.

- **Share Your Progress**: Keep your mentor updated on your achievements and milestones. Letting them see the impact of their guidance reinforces the value of the relationship.

When you engage actively and express gratitude, you strengthen the bond with your mentor and lay the groundwork for a lasting connection.

6. Know When to Evolve the Relationship

Not all mentoring relationships are meant to last forever, and that's okay. As you grow and achieve your goals, the dynamics of your mentorship may naturally shift. Knowing when to evolve or end the relationship is an important part of respecting both your mentor's time and your own development.

- **Reassess Periodically**: Check in with your mentor to evaluate the progress you've made and whether the relationship is still meeting both of your expectations.

- **Transition Gracefully**: If you feel the mentorship has run its course, express your gratitude for their support and keep the door open for future conversations.

- **Stay Connected**: Even if the formal mentorship ends, maintain a connection with your mentor. Share updates on your progress and let them know how their guidance continues to impact your journey.

Recognizing when to evolve the relationship ensures that it remains positive, productive, and respectful.

The Art of Seeking and Engaging with Mentors

Finding and working with a mentor is one of the most impactful steps you can take toward personal and professional growth. By approaching mentorship with intention, clarity, and respect, you can build relationships that provide guidance, encouragement, and opportunities to succeed.

Remember, mentorship is a two-way street—it requires effort, commitment, and genuine connection. When you take the time to seek out the right mentor, set clear expectations, and engage actively, you create a partnership that benefits both of you. So, don't be afraid to reach out, ask for help, and invest in relationships that can transform your journey.

Chapter 15

Let's Sum It Up

As we wrap up this section on mastering your business, it's important to reflect on the journey we've taken together. Business mastery isn't just about building a successful enterprise—it's about creating value, fostering meaningful connections, and leading with purpose and integrity. Whether you're a seasoned entrepreneur, an emerging leader, or someone striving to turn a vision into reality, the principles we've explored provide a framework for long-term growth, influence, and impact.

Let's revisit the key insights from this section and explore how you can take bold steps toward transforming your business and leadership.

Recap of Business Mastery Insights

In Part III, we delved into the foundations of business mastery, covering essential strategies and mindsets that every leader should embrace. Each chapter focused on a core principle designed to help you elevate your approach, lead with confidence, and build a thriving business.

1. Create and Deliver Value (Chapter 11: You Have to Give to Get Value)

At the heart of every successful business is the ability to create and deliver value. It's not enough to sell products or services—you must understand the needs of your customers, employees, and stakeholders and align your efforts with their priorities. When you focus on giving before you get, you build trust, loyalty, and sustainable success.

Key takeaways:

Shift your mindset from transactions to relationships.

Align your solutions with the specific needs of your audience.

Measure and refine your value proposition to stay relevant and impactful.

Creating value isn't just a business strategy—it's a philosophy. It's about serving others, exceeding expectations, and becoming a trusted partner in their success.

2. Redefine Sales as Service (Chapter 12: Selling is Serving)

Selling often gets a bad reputation, but when reframed as an act of service, it becomes one of the most meaningful ways to connect with others and make a difference. Ethical, service-driven sales strategies not only build trust but also create lasting customer relationships.

Key takeaways:

Approach sales with empathy, listening more than you talk.

Tailor your offerings to meet the unique needs of your customers.

Build relationships by focusing on long-term value rather than short-term gains.

When you see selling as an opportunity to serve, it transforms the process into a partnership where both parties succeed.

3. Master Financial Literacy (Chapter 13: Get Your Money Up)

Financial literacy is a cornerstone of business success. Understanding how money works, making informed decisions, and managing resources effectively are essential for both personal and business growth. It's not just about making money—it's about using it wisely to create opportunities and build a secure future.

Key takeaways:

- Create a financial plan that aligns with your goals.

- Diversify your investments to balance risk and maximize returns.

- Use tax-advantaged accounts and strategic planning to grow your wealth.

By mastering financial management, you gain the confidence to lead with clarity and seize opportunities that drive growth.

4. Build Meaningful Connections (Chapter 14: Don't Be Afraid to Ask for Help)

No one succeeds alone. Mentorship and networks are invaluable resources for navigating challenges, finding opportunities, and accelerating your growth. Asking for help is not a sign of weakness—it's a powerful step toward achieving your goals.

Key takeaways:

- Seek out mentors who align with your goals and values.

- Build and nurture a network of genuine, mutually beneficial relationships.

- Engage actively with your mentors and peers, showing gratitude and commitment.

Leaning on the wisdom and support of others helps you avoid pitfalls, gain new perspectives, and achieve more than you ever could alone.

******

Encouragement to Take Bold Steps in Business Transformation

Mastering your business is not about following a one-size-fits-all formula—it's about embracing principles that empower you to lead with purpose, adapt to challenges, and create a lasting impact. The journey requires courage, commitment, and the willingness to step outside your comfort zone. But the rewards are worth it: a thriving business, meaningful relationships, and a legacy of service and success.

As you move forward, remember these guiding principles:

- **Be Purpose-Driven**: Let your vision and values guide your decisions. When you lead with purpose, you inspire trust, loyalty, and passion in those around you.

- **Stay Resilient**: Business is full of ups and downs. Embrace challenges as opportunities to learn, grow, and innovate. Resilience is what turns setbacks into stepping stones.

- **Keep Learning**: The most successful leaders are lifelong learners. Stay curious, seek feedback, and adapt to the ever-changing landscape of business and leadership.

Above all, take bold steps. Whether it's launching a new initiative, reaching out to a mentor, or rethinking your sales strategies, boldness is what propels you forward. It's not about taking reckless risks—it's about having the courage to pursue your vision, even when the path is uncertain.

Moving Forward: Your Business, Your Legacy

As we conclude this section, I want to remind you of the incredible potential you hold as a leader. Mastering your business is not just about achieving financial success—it's about creating value, fostering connections, and making a positive impact in the world.

Take the insights we've explored—creating value, selling with integrity, mastering finances, and building strong relationships—and use them as tools to transform your business and leadership. Lean into the challenges, embrace the opportunities, and never stop striving for excellence.

Your business is more than just a venture—it's a reflection of your purpose, your values, and your legacy. So, take what you've learned, apply it with intention, and watch as your efforts create ripples of impact that go far beyond the bottom line.

Conclusion

As we reach the end of this journey, it's time to reflect on the transformation you've been invited to embrace. This book is more than a guide—it's a call to action for you as a leader to step into your fullest potential by mastering your health, life, and business. Together, we've explored the strategies, mindsets, and practices that will not only elevate your leadership but also help you thrive as a whole person.

Summary of Key Points

We began with the foundation: **Mastering Your Health**. This first part of the book introduced the concept of three-dimensional health—physical, mental, and spiritual well-being—and how their balance is essential for sustainable leadership. You learned that your body is your foundation, your mind is your compass, and your spirit is your anchor. From practical tips for fitness and nutrition to strategies for mental clarity and spiritual grounding, this section equipped you with tools to create a life where you can lead with energy, resilience, and purpose.

We then moved into **Mastering Your Life**, where the focus shifted to creating a life framework that supports leadership success. Simplifying your life through the power of subtraction, setting boundaries, and establishing meaningful routines were all explored as ways to reduce overwhelm and enhance focus. You learned that balance isn't a myth—it's a practice of intentional choices that align your time and energy with what matters most.

Finally, we dove into **Mastering Your Business**, uncovering strategies for building a values-driven enterprise. From creating value for stakeholders to selling as a form of service, this section highlighted the importance of ethical leadership and financial literacy. You discovered the power of mentorship and networks and how asking for help is a strength, not a weakness. These lessons provide a roadmap for leading with integrity and creating impact.

Sustaining Transformation

Transformation isn't a one-time event; it's a continuous process of growth, reflection, and intentional action. The principles outlined in this book are designed to be revisited, adapted, and integrated into every stage of your journey as a leader. Here are a few reminders to help you sustain the transformation you've begun:

1. **Keep Balance at the Forefront**: Regularly assess your physical, mental, and spiritual well-being. When one area feels off, take steps to bring it back into alignment. Remember, leadership starts with leading yourself.

2. **Embrace the Power of Small Steps**: Big changes happen through consistent, small actions. Whether it's a five-minute meditation, a single healthy meal, or a conversation with a mentor, each step you take builds momentum toward lasting growth.

3. **Be Intentional with Your Time**: Leadership is demanding, but your time is your most valuable resource. Regularly revisit your priorities and make sure your schedule reflects what matters most.

4. **Lead with Integrity and Compassion**: Whether in your life or business, stay connected to your values. Lead in a way that inspires trust, cultivates relationships, and leaves a positive impact on those around you.

Leading by Example

The greatest leaders are those who inspire others not just through their words but through their actions. As you embody the principles in this book, you'll set an example for your team, your peers, and your community. When you prioritize your health, balance your life, and lead your business with purpose, you create a ripple effect that encourages others to do the same.

Leadership isn't about perfection—it's about authenticity. It's about showing up, even when it's hard, and committing to growth, even when it's uncomfortable. By embracing the transformation laid out in these pages, you're not just elevating your own life—you're empowering those around you to rise to their fullest potential.

******

Your Next Chapter

Your journey doesn't end here—practically, it's just beginning. Take the lessons, strategies, and inspiration from this book and make them your own. Keep pushing forward, keep growing, and keep showing up as the leader you were meant to be. Remember, transformation is a process, and every step you take brings you closer to the life and leadership you envision.

You have the power to create a life that reflects your values, fulfills your purpose, and inspires those around you. So go out there and lead with strength, clarity, and courage. The world needs your unique vision, your authentic leadership, and the transformation only you can bring.

Appendix A
Resources for Ongoing Growth

Leadership is an ever-evolving journey. The tools, strategies, and insights shared in this book provide a strong foundation, but your growth doesn't stop here. To continue building on what you've learned, it's important to stay curious, seek out new knowledge, and explore resources that can inspire and equip you for the challenges ahead.

Below is a curated list of resources—books, podcasts, courses, and tools—that can support your ongoing growth in health, life, and business. These recommendations are designed to keep you motivated, informed, and empowered to lead with purpose and confidence.

Books to Deepen Your Understanding

- **Health and Wellness**:

    o *Atomic Habits* by James Clear – A practical guide to building habits that stick, perfect for those looking to create lasting change in their health routines.

    o *The Body Keeps the Score* by Bessel van der Kolk – A powerful exploration of how trauma impacts the body and mind, with strategies for healing and resilience.

- **Personal Development**:
  - *The Power of Now* by Eckhart Tolle – A transformative guide to living in the present and finding balance in life.
  - *Daring Greatly* by Brené Brown – A compelling look at vulnerability and its role in leadership, relationships, and personal growth.

- **Business and Leadership**:
  - *Leaders Eat Last* by Simon Sinek – Insights into building trust, inspiring teams, and leading with empathy.
  - *Good to Great* by Jim Collins – A deep dive into what separates successful businesses from the rest and how to create enduring greatness.

Podcasts for Inspiration and Learning

- **The Daily Stoic** – Short, insightful episodes that apply ancient Stoic principles to modern leadership and life.

- **The Tim Ferriss Show** – Interviews with world-class performers that uncover habits, strategies, and tools for success.

- **How I Built This with Guy Raz** – Inspiring stories of entrepreneurs and innovators who turned their ideas into thriving businesses.

- **Unlocking Us with Brené Brown** – Conversations that explore courage, vulnerability, and connection in leadership and life.

*****

Online Courses and Workshops

- **Coursera and edX**: Platforms offering courses from top universities on leadership, financial literacy, mindfulness, and more.

- **LinkedIn Learning**: On-demand video tutorials covering everything from time management to advanced business strategies.

- **MasterClass**: Expert-led classes on topics like communication, negotiation, and personal branding.

*****

Tools for Personal and Professional Growth

- **For Productivity**:

  o Trello or Asana – Project management tools to help you stay organized and focused.

  o Notion – An all-in-one workspace for tracking goals, creating routines, and managing tasks.

- **For Financial Management**:

  o Mint – A personal finance app for budgeting and expense tracking.

  o QuickBooks – Accounting software for managing your business finances.

- **For Mental and Spiritual Well-Being**:

  o Headspace or Calm – Apps for mindfulness and meditation.

  o Gratitude Journal – A simple, powerful way to cultivate positivity and reflection.

Appendix B

Success is rarely achieved in isolation. Your connections—whether mentors, peers, or professional networks—play a crucial role in your journey as a leader. Below are recommended networks, organizations, and communities that can provide support, collaboration opportunities, and access to valuable resources.

Professional Networks

- **National Association for Female Executives (NAFE)**: A supportive network for women in business, offering resources, events, and mentorship opportunities.

- **Young Presidents' Organization (YPO)**: A global network of executives under 45 focused on leadership development and peer learning.

- **Entrepreneur's Organization (EO)**: A community of entrepreneurs dedicated to growing their businesses and supporting each other.

Industry-Specific Organizations

- **For Health and Wellness Professionals**:
    - o American Council on Exercise (ACE) – Certification programs, resources, and a community for health and fitness professionals.

o   Institute for Integrative Nutrition (IIN) – A global network of health coaches and wellness advocates.

- **For Business Leaders**:

   o   SCORE – A nonprofit organization offering free business mentoring and resources for entrepreneurs.

   o   Chamber of Commerce – Local chapters provide networking opportunities and advocacy for businesses in your area.

Mentorship Platforms

- **MentorCity**: An online platform that connects mentors and mentees in various industries.

- **MicroMentor**: A global network that pairs entrepreneurs with experienced business mentors.

Online Communities

- **LinkedIn Groups**:

   o   Women in Leadership – A group for female leaders to connect, share insights, and support one another.

   o   The Leadership Network – A community for discussing leadership trends, challenges, and solutions.

- **Facebook Groups**:

   o   Boss Women Who Brunch – A supportive community for women entrepreneurs and professionals.

   o   Body&Mind Fitness for the 7-figure female leader – Author's FB Group

   o   Creative Entrepreneurs – A space for creative minds to share ideas, collaborate, and grow.

Local and Regional Resources

- **Meetup**: Use this platform to find local groups focused on leadership, entrepreneurship, or industry-specific topics.

- **Alumni Associations**: Connect with fellow graduates from your university or college for networking and professional development opportunities.

- **Toastmasters International**: A global organization that helps individuals improve their public speaking and leadership skills.

*****

These resources and networks are just glimpses of what's available to support your ongoing growth as a leader. The key is to stay engaged, seek out opportunities to learn, and actively connect with people and organizations that inspire you. Remember, growth is a continuous process, and the tools you choose to invest in today will help shape the leader you become tomorrow.

About The Author

Dr. Tasheema Fair is a Health and Wellness Coach dedicated to empowering high-achieving professional women to build the body of their dreams and achieve sustainable results. With her holistic and personalized approach, she guides her clients toward living healthier, more fulfilling lives while embracing their full potential.

A board-certified Obstetrician/Gynecologist, Dr. Fair brings over two decades of medical expertise and a passion for wellness to her practice. As a Colonel in the United States Army Reserves, she exemplifies discipline, leadership, and resilience—qualities she integrates into her coaching to inspire others to overcome challenges and thrive.

Dr. Fair's mission is to help women who value quality prioritize their health, master their mindset, and achieve lasting transformation with precision and purpose.

For inquiries or feedback related to the book:

Email: support@ladydocnutrition.com

"Your journey to transform is a lifelong commitment to growth, balance, and purpose. Go forth boldly, lead authentically, and let your impact inspire others to do the same."

www.ingramcontent.com/pod-product-compliance
Lightning Source LLC
Chambersburg PA
CBHW051200120626
46547CB00012B/1137